I 42

Major General
James Lawson Kemper
C.S.A.

The Confederacy's Forgotten Son

Major General

James Lawson Kemper

C.S.A.

The Confederacy's Forgotten Son

Harold R. Woodward, Jr.

Rockbridge Publishing Company
Natural Bridge Station, Virginia

Published by

Rockbridge Publishing Company
Post Office Box 70
Natural Bridge Station, VA 24579
Telephone: 703-291-1063
Facsimile: 703-291-1346

Library of Congress Cataloging-in-Publication Data

Woodward, Harold R.
    Major General James Lawson Kemper, C.S.A. : the Confederacy's forgotten
son / Harold R. Woodward, Jr. — 1st ed.
    p.   cm.
    Includes bibliographical references and index.
    ISBN 0-9623572-7-8
    1. Kemper, James Lawson, 1823-1985.   2. Generals—Confederate States
of America—Biography.   3. Confederate States of America. Army—
Biography.   4. Confederate States of America. Army. Virginia Infantry
Regiment, 7th.   5. Governors—Virginia—Biography.
I. Title
E467.1.K3W66   1993
973.7'455—dc20   93-22486
                                                              CIP

10 9 8 7 6 5 4 3 2 1
First Edition

"Poor is a nation that has no heroes. Poorer still is one that has them and forgets them."

— Winston Churchill

Table of Contents

Dedication ix

Acknowledgements xi

Introduction xiii

Chapter 1   *On the Old Plantation*..........................   1

Chapter 2   *Building of a Career*   6

Chapter 3   *The Mexican War*.................................   9

Chapter 4   *The Country Lawyer*   16

Chapter 5   *The Young Politician*...........................   20

Chapter 6   *The Coming Struggle*   24

Chapter 7   *Secession*......................................   30

Chapter 8   *The Seventh Virginia Regiment*..................   37

Chapter 9   *First Taste of Battle*..........................   42

Chapter 10   *Grim Reality*   47

Chapter 11   *The Peninsula Campaign*   52

Chapter 12   *Manassas to Maryland and Back*.................   63

Chapter 13   *The Winter of 1862-63*   72

Chapter 14   *The North Carolina Campaign*   79

Chapter 15   *The March Northward*   84

Chapter 16   *"The Sun was Darkened"*.........................   89

Chapter 17   *Nothing But Glory*   94

Chapter 18   *Aftermath of the Battle*   99

Chapter 19   *Return to Duty*.................................   105

Chapter 20   *The Last Days of the Confederacy*.............   113

Chapter 21   *Beginning Anew*   117

Chapter 22   *Business Ventures*. 123

Chapter 23   *The Country Lawyer Resumes His Practice* 128

Chapter 24   *Return to Politics* 133

Chapter 25   *The Conservatives Become Effective*. 137

Chapter 26   *The Road to the Governor's Office*. 143

Chapter 27   *The Nomination for Governor* 149

Chapter 28   *The Election of 1873* 155

Chapter 29   *The First Year of Kemper's Administration* 163

Chapter 30   *Kemper and the Public Debt* 172

Chapter 31   *The Second and Third Years* 176

Chapter 32   *Final Year as Governor* 182

Chapter 33   *Return to Private Life* 185

Chapter 34   *End of the Line* 191

Bibliography and Sources. 197

Index   205

About the Author 215

Dedication

This book is dedicated to all the men of the Kemper-Fry-Strother Camp No. 19, Sons of Confederate Veterans, Madison, Virginia, who keep history alive with pride.

Acknowledgements

So many people and institutions have helped in one way or another or lent support and encouragement to this project that I am afraid that I may forget someone's contribution here. If I have done so, it was not intentional, and I hope no one feels slighted. I want everyone who helped in any way to know how much I appreciate what you have done.

I want to thank the following individuals for their help: my good friend Steve Hoffman, Mr. and Mrs. I. W. Jeannes, Judge and Mrs. Basil Burke, Jr., Nancy DeJarnette Berry, John Dwyer, Dr. Gene Harris and his dear wife Jan, Ernie Runyon, Bob Ward, John Hightower, Leri Thomas, Darrell Estes, Kathie Tennery, Garth Kemper, Crosby Kemper, Phyllis Woodward and, most of all, my loyal typist, Audrey Sarate.

By far the biggest help of all were the three institutions that have maintained and preserved Kemper's personal and official papers: the Alderman Library at the University of Virginia, the Virginia State Historical Society, and the Virginia State Library.

I wish also to acknowledge the help of the following libraries and institutions: The Madison County Public Library, Orange County Public Library, Madison Heritage Foundation, Orange County Historical Society, James Madison Regional Library, Albemarle Historical Society, Culpeper Town and County Library, the Preston Library at Virginia Military Institute, the University of Richmond Library, Washington and Lee University Library, Woodberry Forest School Library, Virginia Polytechnic Institute and State University Library, and the Museum of the Confederacy.

Also of great help were the following: the Orange County Circuit Court Clerk's Office, the Madison County Circuit Court Clerk's Office, the National Archives, the Fredericksburg National Military Park, the Gettysburg National Battlefield Park, Antietam National Battlefield Park, and the Manassas National Battlefield Park.

Introduction

Service to the state is a time honored and well respected tradition among Virginians. James Lawson Kemper is the epitome of what service to state truly means. From the halls of the state legislature, to the field of combat as an officer in the Confederate Army, and finally as Governor of Virginia, Kemper dedicated the bigger part of his life to serving Virginia and Virginians. And though honorably he served, for some reason his biography has never been written. His nephew, W. Kemper Bocock, started one in the 1890s, but never got around to completing it. Some historians have mentioned his civilian accomplishments, and others have written of his military commands, but none have written about the man.

It may well be that his accomplishments in the state legislature before the war were overshadowed by the terrible events that followed. His military record during his Confederate service is perhaps dwarfed by such legendary figures as Lee, Jackson, and Stuart. And his term as governor, although during one of history's most trying times, is very complicated and follows too closely an event of such magnitude that it is overlooked in the whole picture of Virginia's history.

It is, therefore, with a great deal of pride that I present this book on a man who is Madison County's most famous son and the Confederacy's forgotten son: James Lawson Kemper.

The inspiration to do this book came from my love of history and my deep involvement in the Sons of Confederate Veterans. Confederate Generals have been favorite topics of biographies, especially those in Lee's Army of Northern Virginia. I was, therefore, dismayed to find that so little was written on Kemper.

It is hard to believe that a man who contributed so much is largely forgotten, although his virtual obscurity is being somewhat overcome today. His home is undergoing massive restoration using private and public funds. It is hoped, when completed, that the Kemper Mansion will be a showcase for Madison County history with strong emphasis on its most famous occupant. Annual commemorations are being held at his gravesite on his birthday by the Kemper-Fry-Strother Camp No. 19 of the Sons of Confederate Veterans that in part bears his name. The new bridge on U.S. Route 15 across the Rapidan River is named in his honor.

My sole goal is doing this book is so that future generations will have a means of remembering a truly remarkable man. My sole wish is that I have accomplished that goal.

Harold R. Woodward, Jr.
Madison, Virginia
25 February 1993

Chapter 1

On the Old Plantation

Mountain Prospect was the Kemper family plantation at the foot of towering Thoroughfare Mountain in northern Madison County, Virginia. William Kemper bought this land and began a plantation here in 1800. It was here he brought his bride, Maria E. Allison, in 1802, and it was here that James Lawson Kemper was born on June 11, 1823, the sixth of eight children.[1]

James Lawson Kemper traced his paternal ancestors from Müson, a small village in southwestern Germany, about fifteen miles northeast of Siegen. His great-great-great-grandfather, John George Kemper, the son of Johann and Ann Löw Kemper, was an elder in the German Reformed Church and a proficient blacksmith and iron worker.

Kemper's great-great-grandfather, John Kemper, a man of some

---

1. Kemper's siblings: I. **Mary Allison** m. Arthur Freeman; nine children. II. **Frederick Thomas** (1816-1881) m. Susan Holton Taylor; eleven children. III. **William Henry** (1819-1843) n.m. IV. **Susan Elizabeth** (1820-1875) m. Oliver Matthews; three children. V. **John Stadler** (1823-1887) n.m. VI. **James Lawson.** VII. **Maria Rebecca** (1825-1873) m. William F. Botts; eight children. VIII. **Sarah Margaret** m. Rev. John Holmes Bocock D.D; five children. [Vee Dove, *Madison County Homes: A Collection of Pre-Civil War Homes and Family Heritage* (Kingsport, Tennessee, 1975) pp. 64-65]

learning and very well thought of in the community, emigrated to Virginia in 1714 as one of forty miners procured by Baron de Graffenuid for the iron mines at Governor Alexander Spotswood's colony at Germanna.[2] Kemper's great-grandfather, John Peter Kemper, was born at Germanna, but in the 1720s the family moved to Fauquier County, Virginia, where they established Cedar Grove, a thriving plantation of over a thousand acres near Germantown.

Kemper's grandfather, Frederick Kemper, grew up in a home where German was spoken; he attended the German Reformed Church, where services were held in German. He died from a fall from a horse in 1783, leaving a wife, five daughters and one son.[3]

The son, William Kemper, moved to Madison County, Virginia, in the late 1790s and established himself as a merchant in the new town of Madison Court House.[4] On March 15 and December 19, 1800, for a total investment of $5,541.40, he acquired more than 900 acres of land that were the basis for his Mountain Prospect plantation.[5]

On his mother's side, James Kemper was descended from John Jasper Stadler, who had planned the fortifications for Maryland, Virginia, and North Carolina during the Revolutionary War as a colonel of engineers on George Washington's staff. For his efforts, Col. Stadler was awarded a considerable amount of land in Kentucky by a grateful nation.[6] The colonel's daughter, Mary Dorothea Stadler, married Thomas Lawson Allison. Their son, John Stadler Allison, was an officer in the War of 1812. Their daughter, Maria

---

2.   Robert Rivers Jones, "Forgotten Virginian: The Early Life and Career of James Lawson Kemper, 1823-1865" (University of Virginia: Master Thesis, Charlottesville, Virginia, 1961) pp. 3-9.
3.   *Ibid.*, p. 18.
4.   Madison County had been formed in 1792 and the county seat was established in 1793.
5.   Jones, "Forgotten Virginian" p. 18.
6.   *Ibid.*, p. 13.

E. Allison, who lost her father when she was very young, married William Kemper in 1802.

Mountain Prospect was a typical plantation of the period, said to resemble a small English village on a mighty hill.[7] Besides the main house, which has a panoramic view of the Blue Ridge Mountains, the dependencies included a smaller brick cottage, carriage house, dairy, summer house, barn, tobacco barn, meathouse and several slave cabins. Nearby was a grist mill, shoemaker's shop, smithy and carpenter's shop. Also nearby was the school building and a small family graveyard.[8]

The main house is brick with a high pitched roof and twin chimneys on one end. The fireplaces have large, ornate mantles. There is a grand entrance hall and formal parlor and dining room. The house was well-planned and built of the finest materials with a high level of craftsmanship and a great deal of manual labor.[9]

The soils of the plantation were fertile and well suited for tobacco, hay and grains. The pastures provided excellent grazing for cattle. The forests contained mature stands of the finest oak, pine, hickory, walnut, ash, locust and poplar timber.

Typical plantation life in antebellum Virginia was a "beautiful and enjoyable life . . . it was a soft, dreamy, deliciously quiet life, a life of repose, an old life, with all its sharp corners and rough surfaces long ago worn round and smooth."[10]

Virginians of the time enjoyed an "idleness and freedom from business cares and a climate so perfect that existence itself was a luxury within their borders. Habits and customs found good were retained."[11]

---

7.   Dove, p. 65.
8.   *Ibid.*, p. 65; Jones, "Forgotten Virginian," p. 28.
9.   The house today is the home of Judge and Mrs. Basil Burke, Jr. [Dove, p. 65].
10.   George A. Eggleston, *A Rebel's Recollections* (Bloomington, 1957).
11.   *Ibid.*

Young James spent his childhood amid an extended family on the plantation. Besides his parents and siblings, four of his father's sisters and his maternal grandmother lived at Mountain Prospect, as well as several domestic servants.[12] Their life revolved around church and home. James's mother was deeply religious; his father was an elder in the Presbyterian church. Maria Kemper was fond of music and young people, and the Kempers hosted dances and parties that often lasted several days. The boys played croquet and town ball, an old game similar to baseball; the girls took part in quilting and rug making.[13]

William Kemper was a knowledgeable man who loved the land, and the plantation was almost completely self-sufficient. All the food was grown there except for tea, coffee, sugar and salt. The nearest market was Fredericksburg, some forty miles and nearly a week away by wagon because of the poor roads. A trip to market was a rare chance to witness outside life. Another opportunity to garner an education off of the plantation were the March Court Days at Madison Court House. While court was in session, peddlers hawked their wares and the gentlemen talked of politics and military matters.[14]

Young James's first formal education came when his father and a neighboring planter, Colonel Henry Hill of Culpeper, formed the Old Field School on the Kemper plantation for educating their own children.[15] One boyhood friendship that would last nearly a lifetime was formed with Colonel Hill's son, Ambrose Powell Hill.[16]

From 1830 to 1840, age seven to seventeen, James boarded at

---

12. Jones, "Forgotten Virginian," pp. 19-23.
13. *Ibid.*, p. 26.
14. Jones, "Forgotten Virginian," p. 29.
15. *Ibid.*, p. 31.
16. Hill also became a Confederate General. [James I. Robertson, Jr. *General A. P. Hill: the story of a Confederate Warrior* (New York), 1987) p. 6].

the Locust Dale Academy, a nearby school for boys that ran from September until June.[17] The boys lived two to a room in two-story dormitories. The school had a military corps of cadets, and in addition to numerous academic subjects, military training was compulsory. Uniformed parades and drills were part of daily routine. Upon graduation a young man was eligible for acceptance at several fine schools of higher education including Washington College in Lexington, Virginia.[18]

17.   *Ibid.*, p. 32.
18.   John Edward Dwyer, "A Historical Survey of Changes in Education in Madison County 1792-1970" (University of Richmond: Master Thesis, Richmond, Virginia, 1970) pp. 29-30.

Chapter 2

Building a Career

James Lawson Kemper arrived at Lexington to begin classes at Washington College in late August 1840. The college, founded by Presbyterian settlers in 1749 and named for the nation's first president, had become one of the state's finest institutions of higher education.

The school consisted of four departments: classical, mathematical, physical science and rhetorical and ethical. Courses in agriculture were also offered. There were very strict regulations against drinking, gambling, profanity and dancing. School began September 1 and classes, small in size, lasted from dawn to dusk. A typical day began with chapel services at 5:00 AM. There were three examination periods during the school year. The only break the students received was a nine-day recess at Christmas. Commencement was held the last Thursday in June. Tuition was forty dollars per year. Room, board, washing, firewood, and candles added another $150.00.[1]

Kemper joined the Washington Literary Society, the school's debating society. Its members debated such issues as religion, education, literature and civics. Emphasis was put on public speaking.

---

1.   Jones, "Forgotten Virginian," p. 34.

Students who participated and did well left well suited for a career in politics or public service.

Neighboring Virginia Military Institute offered students at Washington College the opportunity to take military instruction. Kemper attended the class conducted by the Cincinnati Professor of Military Science that emphasized civil engineering.

The Cincinnati School of Military Science, named for the Roman patriot who was the citizen-soldier role model, was a school within a school. The Cincinnati cadets wore military uniforms, were trained in the use of military equipment, and held dress parades and drilled daily from noon until 1:00 PM.[2]

Kemper was studious, a hard worker, and was well thought of by his fellow students. Among his classmates were John Letcher of Lexington, a future governor of Virginia; John D. Imboden of Augusta County, who would become a general in the Confederate army; John C. Rutherford of Goochland County, who was destined to become an influential legislator; and John H. McCue of Augusta County, who would become a district judge in Staunton.[3]

A few days before his nineteenth birthday, in the spring of 1842, Washington College awarded Kemper a Bachelor of Arts degree. Kemper gave the commencement address at his graduation. His topic was "The Need of a Public School System in Virginia."[4]

After graduation Kemper returned home to Mountain Prospect where he contemplated attending the University of Virginia Law School. At that time he joined the "Tee-Total Society," a local group of young men opposed to alcoholic drink.[5]

He eventually accepted an invitation to study law under the Honorable George W. Summers of Charleston, Kanawha County (now West Virginia). Judge Summers, also a graduate of Washing-

2. *Ibid.*, p. 41.
3. *Ibid.*, p. 36.
4. *Ibid.*, p. 41.
5. *Ibid.*, p. 42.

ton College, was a most-respected and well-liked jurist and a member of the United States House of Representatives.[6] After completing his studies under Judge Summers, Kemper was granted a Master's Degree by Washington College in June 1845.[7]

Kemper then returned to Madison County, where he applied for a license to practice law. He was admitted to the bar October 2, 1846, and then opened a law practice [8]

Kemper was young, healthy, intelligent and well educated. He was broad-shouldered, thick-chested, had thick black hair, a high forehead and large brown eyes.[9] He was a young man expecting to settle into a worthy career in his home town, but his plans were soon interrupted. Congress declared war against Mexico on May 13, 1846. In early December President James Polk called for nine regiments of volunteers from the several states. The First Regiment of Virginia Volunteers was being organized, and several openings for officers still existed. Kemper decided to try his luck at getting a commission to fill one of those positions.[10]

---

6.   *Ibid.*, p. 43.
7.   *Ibid.*, p. 44.
8.   Papers of James Lawson Kemper, Virginia Historical Society, Richmond, Virginia (hereafter referred to as V.H.S.): License to practice law.
9.   Jones, "Forgotten Virginian," p. 45.
10.   "The Mexican War Diary of James Lawson Kemper" by Robert R. Jones, *The Virginia Magazine of History and Biography* vol. 74 no. 4 October 1966, p. 387. (Hereafter referred to as Mexican War Diary.)

Chapter 3

The Mexican War

Kemper boarded a stage for the nation's capital on December 15, 1846, in hopes of securing a commission in the First Regiment of Virginia Volunteers.[1] The First Virginia was nearly complete; five of the six companies had already rendezvoused at Richmond and embarked for Fortress Monroe.[2]

Kemper's companion on the trip to Washington was Birkett Davenport Fry of Kanawha County.[3] (Fry would become a brigadier general in the Confederate army.) Kemper suffered from motion sickness on the long, rough trip over the poor roads of the time. They reached their destination on December 20. Kemper began to keep a diary.[4]

On December 20, Kemper and Fry called on Henry Hill of Culpeper County in the Navy Department, and congressman Shelton F. Leake, a Democrat from Charlottesville. Both men promised to do all they could to help the young commission seekers. On December 22, they saw Judge John Y. Mason, the secretary of the

---

1. Mexican War Diary, p. 387.
2. *Washington Daily National Intelligencer* January 4, 1847.
3. Mexican War Diary, p. 390.
4. The diary now in the Kemper papers at V.H.S. was referred to by him as his journal.

Navy and a personal friend of President Polk. They then visited Governor William L. March, the Secretary of War, who complimented both men on their appearance and assured them that their claims were strong. They learned that openings existed as assistant quartermaster and assistant commissary, and they stood good chances of getting them.[5]

On Wednesday December 23, Kemper boarded the steamer *Powhatan* bound for Richmond. He had decided to seek support for his appointment from some of the influential men there. He reached Richmond at 10:00 PM on Thursday and spent the night at the Powhatan House, one of the capital city's finest hotels. The next morning he witnessed Captain Scott's company, the Richmond Grays, drilling. He went to see Charles Dorman, an influential member of the House of Delegates and a brigadier general in the Virginia Militia, and spent Christmas Day with General Dorman and his family. Other guests that day included General William Richardson, adjutant-general of Virginia; Governor William "Extra-Billy" Smith; and many members of the General Assembly.[6] Kemper made friends easily and gained a great deal of encouragement.

Kemper returned to Washington on December 27. He immediately set about contacting the members of Virginia's congressional delegation. He met and pleaded his case with Senator Augustus Alexander Chapman of Union; representatives Henry Bedinger of Charlestown; former governor, now representative, James McDowell of Lexington; Edmund Wilcox Hubbard of Cardsville; Thomas H. Bagby of Accomack; William Marshall Treadway of Danville; and James Alexander Seddon of Richmond.[7] (Representative Sed-

5.   Mexican War Diary, p. 390. Washington, D.C. retained a small town atmosphere, it is incomprehensible today that two virtual unknowns could make such contacts.
6.   Mexican War Diary, p. 391.
7.   *Ibid.*, p. 392.

don would go on to become the Confederate Secretary of War.) He also met President Polk and Secretary of State James Buchanan, both of whom received him very graciously.[8]

While in Washington he attended many sessions of Congress. After hearing Senator John Caldwell Calhoun of South Carolina make a speech on the floor of the Senate, he remarked, "What a man!"[9] He also met Colonel Joseph Eggleston Johnston (a future Confederate general) who delivered to him the news of his appointment as quartermaster with the First Virginia.[10]

On January 5, 1847, Kemper received his first instruction on the duties of a quartermaster and was bonded for the amount of $10,000.00.[11]

Kemper formed some good opinions on proper public speaking after hearing some of the sessions in Congress. "The truth is, these members don't know when they are done speaking. . . . They don't recollect that the great men of the first Congress rarely spoke more than ten minutes," he wrote.[12]

It is amazing the number of people Kemper became acquainted with during such a short stay in Washington. He met Captain Samuel H. Walker of the Texas Rangers, designer of the Colt-Walker revolver and hero of the Texas War for Independence; Senator Robert A. Toombs of Georgia, (future Confederate cabinet member and Confederate general) whom he described as "a right good speaker"; and Senator Daniel Webster, the great statesman from Boston and famed orator, whom he noted was the "greatest man in *appearance* I ever saw."[13]

He also heard some of the debate over the slavery question

---

8. *Ibid.*, p. 393.
9. *Ibid.*, p. 394.
10. *Ibid.*, p. 394.
11. *Ibid.*, p. 395.
12. *Ibid.*, p. 396.
13. *Ibid.*, pp. 397-401.

which was going on in Congress at the time. He heard Representative John Pettit of Indiana call slavery a "moral, political, and physical evil." Representative Pettit opposed the expansion of slavery "under any circumstance." On the other side of the issue he heard Representative Robert Barnwell Rhett of South Carolina argue the virtues of states' rights, southern rights, and a proposal to extend the Missouri Compromise line. He also heard his friend Shelton Leake prophesy the coming struggle in a speech on slavery: "[T]he House seems to have been converted into a magnificent abolition society," he said, and issued "the ultimatum of the South. [If the actions of Congress break in] like an avalanche on the peace and security of the entire South, . . . the South must stand in self-defense."[14]

While waiting for Congress to confirm his appointment as captain of volunteers, Kemper continued to meet influential people and make friends. Among those were Sam Houston of Texas (who was born in Virginia), Stephen Douglas of Illinois, and several future Confederates: Patrick Henry Aylett, later to be Confederate district attorney; Robert M. T. Hunter, future Confederate secretary of state; James Murray Mason, future Confederate diplomat famous in the *Trent* affair; and James E. Slaughter of Culpeper, future brigadier general in the Confederate army.[15]

On February 1, 1847, the Senate confirmed Kemper's appointment to the rank of captain. On February 7, he left Washington for Richmond by steamer, then from Richmond by rail to Old Point Comfort and Fortress Monroe. Here he met his commander, Colonel John Hamtranck. He roomed at Fortress Monroe with the adjutant of the regiment, Major Jubal Anderson Early.[16] The regiment left Fortress Monroe for Mexico aboard the steamer *Exact* on February 21. On the long ocean voyage, Kemper suffered from

14.   *Ibid.*, p. 403.
15.   *Ibid.*, pp. 404-414.
16.   Early became a lieutenant general in the Confederate army.

sea-sickness. His journal tells how he longed for the cool waters of the streams on Thoroughfare Mountain. On the 23rd they passed Cape Hatteras, rounded the Florida coast on the 27th, and on March 4 they caught a glimpse of Cuba. On March 10 they reached Mexico, landing at Brazos.[17]

The Battle of Buena Vista had just ended. The Virginia Regiment was ordered to Monterey and reached the handsome old city after a long hard march through the desert. Kemper and his fellow Virginians were enchanted by the romance of Old Mexico and the peculiar charms of the beautiful countryside with its shaded groves of live oaks, the pecan trees and the cool clean water. They were impressed with Mexican culture, the good wine, the bright flowers, the gaily plumed birds and the fresh fruit. The people were pleasant and friendly. Kemper was intrigued with the huge, beautiful Catholic churches.[18]

The regiment was stationed at Saltillo and Buena Vista in the Province of Coaluila. Their duty was to maintain the defensive perimeter of Parras, Buena Vista, Saltillo and Monterey. They drilled daily and settled into a dull routine camp life. Other than occasional guerilla action against them, there was little excitement.[19]

Morale and discipline became very hard to maintain. Kemper was a fine soldier by all standards and did his best to instill good discipline among the men. Colonel Hamtranck particularly appreciated Kemper's service as this letter to the young captain attests:

> If an undivided devotion to the service of your country, in a perilous, trying, difficult, hazardous, fatiguing, vexatious, long campaign of more than fifteen months has any claim upon the gratitude of your countrymen, you are amply entitled to it.

17.   *Ibid.*, pp. 417-428.
18.   Jones, "Forgotten Virginian," p. 51.
19.   *Ibid.*, pp. 51-53.

Among the pleasing reminiscences of our campaign, none is more refreshing than your conduct in Mexico. You were never seen to play—but early and late, on the march or in camp, in storm or in shine, in all weather and at all times I ever found you at your post—intent at any & every sacrifice of life, limb, and health upon your duty. So distinguished had you become in the line of your particular department that I had some trouble in preventing you being detailed by the Genl. Commanding for duty in a larger sphere—more responsible but less exposed and hazardous. I thought your services however necessary to the Va. Regt., and that body—distinguished for good officers, all well instructed, well equipped, disciplined and ready for action—could not spare you without detriment.[20]

In a later letter, Col. Hamtranck noted that Kemper had "performed the complex and important duties of his position in the army with much success and given 'unusual satisfaction'."[21]

Kemper continued to make influential acquaintances while in the army. He became particularly well acquainted with a future United States president, General Zachary Taylor. After the war, Kemper delighted in telling of General Taylor rushing into his tent one night scared practically to death, fearing he had been bitten by a tarantula. They all had a good laugh when it was discovered that he had only pricked himself on a cactus.[22]

Kemper also became acquainted with Captain Braxton Bragg (later a Confederate general) and Colonel Jefferson Davis (later president of the Confederate States of America). He also got to know John Ellis Wool (later a major general in the union army and

---

20. Papers of James Lawson Kemper, University of Virginia Library, Charlottesville, Virginia (hereafter referred to as Kemper papers, U.Va.) letter of September 21, 1850.
21. *Ibid.*, letter of September 26, 1850.
22. Jones, "Forgotten Virginian," p. 57.

commander of Fortress Monroe), Irwin McDowell (commander of the union army at the first battle of Manassas), and Philip St. George Cocke (father-in-law of James E.B. Stuart and a union general).[23]

On August 3, 1848, James Lawson Kemper was honorably discharged from the United States Army.[24] He then returned to Madison and his law practice.

Kemper's military experience was to prove important to him in later years. Although he didn't obtain the battlefield experience of some other future Confederate or union officers, he did learn a great deal about military life and he learned to work efficiently and effectively under dangerous wartime conditions.

23. *Ibid.*, p. 58.
24. *Ibid.*, p. 59.

Chapter 4

The Country Lawyer

Upon his return to Madison, James Lawson Kemper immediately resumed his law practice. With his oratorical powers and skill in the courtroom, in no time at all he had built up a considerable practice. Judging by the large number of cases he represented, he soon became one of the most sought after attorneys in the area.[1]

He practiced law primarily in his native Madison County and neighboring Orange and Culpeper counties, but as his reputation grew, so did the demand for his services. He was soon traveling throughout the state to represent his many clients. Travel at that time in Virginia was often difficult, and Kemper used the best means available, frequently riding horseback. On long trips he traveled by stagecoach, canal boat or by rail.[2]

When the young attorney's financial condition improved, he purchased a horse drawn buggy for $145, which quickly became his most prized possession.[3] In keeping with his success, by 1850 Kemper owned 200 acres of land in Madison County and a house

---

1. Kemper papers, U.Va.
2. Jones, "Forgotten Virginian," p. 59.
3. *Ibid.*, p. 70. This carriage was probably bought from the Fishback Wagon Factory in Madison.

16

and lot in the town.[4]

At this point, unfortunately, his health began to deteriorate. Certainly the fast pace and pressures of a busy career exacerbated his condition, but the underlying cause for his poor state of health at this time was probably some fever or disease picked up while in Mexico.[5] Off and on for the next several years, Kemper fought bouts of sickness.

Professionally, Kemper was especially active in helping to settle bounty claims for veterans of the War of 1812 and the Mexican War. The government, in return for war service, gave veterans land claims in the western states and territories. In addition to settling claims, Kemper also made a small fortune in land speculation. By buying claims and then selling them for a considerable profit, he was able to accumulate quite a large amount of money for a man of his age.[6]

Another area that interested him was transportation. Roads were practically non-existent and as the need to get agricultural commodities to market grew, the demand for decent roads did likewise. In late 1849, some enterprising men of Madison, Orange and Page counties met, with encouragement from the state, to discuss building a highway from the Shenandoah valley to the rail and market center at Gordonsville. On February 9, 1850, these men met at Madison Court House, formed the Blue Ridge Turnpike Company, and elected a board of directors from among the most prominent citizens of these three counties. Kemper was selected as legal counsel for this board. Shares of stock were sold at $50 each. Kemper became a substantial stockholder.[7]

Survey and examination of the route began almost immediately following the initial meeting. The road was to run from Gor-

---

4. *Ibid.*, p. 70.
5. *Ibid.*, p. 76.
6. *Ibid.*, p. 74.
7. "The Blue Ridge Turnpike Story" by Harold R. Woodward, Jr.

donsville to the intersection with the Sperryville-New Market Turnpike at the base of Massanutten Mountain, a length of fifty-six and one quarter miles. Grading, bridging and macadamizing began on July 15, 1850. The first annual meeting of the board of directors was held at Madison Court House on May 2, 1851. On October 31, 1851, a report was sent to the state Board of Public Works in Richmond, emphasizing the importance of the road as a vital link between the fertile Shenandoah valley and the railroad at Gordonsville. By October 29, 1852, the president of the company was able to report that twenty-two miles of the Blue Ridge Turnpike from Gordonsville to the Blue Ridge Mountains was complete and in good order for travel. Upon completion, the total cost of construction was $176,043.89. The Commonwealth of Virginia owned 2,000 shares in the company, and individuals owned 1,300.[8]

The young lawyer was very interested in politics, and in 1850, when only 27 years old, he sought election as clerk of the state's constitutional convention. Although he was largely unknown across the state, Kemper relied on his Washington College acquaintances, his military experience and his successful law practice to carry his election. Even though he aligned himself solidly with the Democratic Party of the state and had many powerful friends (such as John S. Barbour, the influential Democrat from Culpeper County; Henry Shackelford, state senator from Culpeper Court House; Marcus Newman, delegate in the state legislature from Madison County; Representative Paulus Powell of Amherst County; and General Robert Adam Banks of Madison), he narrowly lost the election.[9]

About this time Kemper began to court young Cremora Conway Cave. Belle, as she was known, was the sixteen-year-old daughter of Belfield Cave, one of the most influential men of the county and

---

8. *Ibid.*
9. Jones, "Forgotten Virginian," p. 108.

long-time clerk of the circuit court.[10] The young couple was married at Madison Court House on July 4, 1853 by the Reverend J. Earnest of Orange Court House.[11]

The young lawyer and family man, although very busy, kept close ties with his family, helping brothers, sisters and parents with legal matters and advice. On October 29, 1853, his father passed away at the age of 76, and it was James's duty to settle the estate.[12]

Undaunted by losing the election for clerk of the constitutional convention, Kemper set about promoting himself as the pro-slave, anti-abolitionist, pro-states' rights challenger for Marcus Newman's seat in the House of Delegates. He became an avid supporter of Henry A. Wise and gained support for his bid for the legislature. After much urging by supporters, he announced his candidacy early in 1853.[13]

10.   Dove, p. 272.
11.   Jones, "Forgotten Virginian," p. 124; Willis Miller Kemper and Henry Lynn Wright, *Genealogy of the Kemper Family of the United States, Descendants of John Kemper of Virginia: With a Short Historical Sketch of His Family and of the German Reformed Colony at Germanna and Germantown, Virginia* (Chicago, Illinois, 1899) the Kempers' children were: I. **Mead Cave** (?-1886) m. Alice Constance Taylor; II. **Frances Merriweather** (died during war); III. **Florence** (1-25-1859 to 1-3-1944) m. John P. (Jack) Thompson; IV. **James Lawson, Jr.** (disappeared about 1890); V. **Lucy Virginia** (? to 12-23-1915, aged 55) m. Dr. Junius F. Lynch at Walnut Hills 12-9-1891, one child, a daughter, Virginia Kemper b. Nov. 1893; VI. **Jessie McRae** d. 8-27-1892, nm.; VII. **Reginald Heber Johns** (9-8-1870 to ?) m. Lucile Amelia DeNormadie.
12.   Kemper papers, U.Va.
13.   *Ibid.*, pp. 117-118.

Chapter 5

The Young Politician

The election for the House of Delegates of 1853 was the most bitter and vindictive that Madison County had ever known.[1]

During the election year, Kemper became involved in a "fierce and embittered feud . . . between wealthy parties," the court case of *Graves v. Early*. Kemper was the legal counsel for Dr. George Nathaniel Thrift (a highly respected medical doctor, who owned Woodbourne Plantation near the town of Madison) and his two nephews.[2]

The simple question, "Whose overcoat have you got on?" may or may not have been asked, but it caused quite a ruckus and nearly ended in a duel. The question, if asked, would show improper influence, as the answer would reveal that the plaintiff's witness was wearing an overcoat belonging to the defendant.[3]

Kemper maintained that Thrift had asked him to ask the question during the course of testimony, and that he (Kemper) considered it insulting and refused to do so. Thrift denied the accusation

---

1. The contest was so bitter and the people of the county so split in loyalty, it is still spoken of today, 139 years later!
2. Jones, "Forgotten Virginian," p. 132; Dove, p. 11.
3. "Courthouses of Madison County" by William H.B. Thomas "Virginia Cavalcade" vol. XIX no. 4 Spring 1970, p. 16.

and responded that the question was Kemper's idea. Kemper considered Thrift's denial an accusation that he had lied. This led to a heated flow of correspondence between the two and their respective followers.[4]

Kemper charged that while on his honeymoon in the late summer of 1853, Thrift had traveled throughout the county slandering him and turning public opinion against him. In late September, Kemper published a pamphlet telling his side of the affair. On October 11, Thrift answered with his own pamphlet.[5]

Kemper was so angered by Thrift's response that he sent Thrift a letter demanding "an affair of honor" take place at daybreak on October 12 in the meadow of Hiram Yager on the banks of White Oak Run.[6]

Judge Richard H. Field, hearing of the affair and "having good cause to suspect that James Lawson Kemper and George Nathaniel Thrift of this county are about to be engaged in a duel," issued bench warrants for their arrest, intending to require them to post bond to keep the peace and not to violate the anti-dueling law. Kemper was required to post a $6,000 bond. He refused to do so and the sheriff was ordered to take him into custody. While being escorted across the court green by the sheriff, Kemper bolted from custody, ran to a horse supplied by his brother John and rode to freedom.[7]

On October 15, Thrift was arrested and on October 18, Kemper was arrested and brought before the judge. They both posted bond and the duel never took place; however, the county was divided by

4. *Ibid.*
5. Jones, "Forgotten Virginian," p. 134; James Lawson Kemper *A History of the Late Difficulties* (Washington, D.C., 1853); George N. Thrift *A Reply* (Washington, D.C., 1854).
6. "Virginia Cavalcade," Spring 1970, p. 16; Jones, "Forgotten Virginian," p. 134.
7. *Ibid.*, p. 16; Jones, "Forgotten Virginian," p. 135; Dove, p. 11.

the affair. Kemper had numerous influential friends who sided with him against Thrift. His leading supporters were his father-in-law Belfield Cave, Commonwealth's Attorney Angus R. Blakey, General Robert Adam Banks, and statesenator Thomas N. Welch. Among Thrift's supporters and his intended second in the duel was Lieutenant-Governor Shelton F. Leake, the former congressman who had helped Kemper to get a commission in the Mexican War and who would become a bitter enemy. The citizens of the county took sides and the pro-Kemper and pro-Thrift factions would oppose one another for years to come.[8]

In 1854, the New York author Horne Tooke published a pamphlet, *Whose Overcoat Have You Got On?*, in which he ridiculed both parties. In it the author proclaimed, "I want them to act towards me as they have towards each other: talk big, talk loud, and look as if they were breathing thunderbolts and had breakfasted upon fried lightening." He concluded his little book by posing the following question, "Now my fellow citizens, is it not clear the question has not yet been spoken to? After all the talking, writing, and printing we have not yet been informed, 'Whose overcoat have you got on?'"[9]

Kemper arrived in Richmond the first week of December 1853 to begin his legislative career. He took up residence at the Powhatan House. The legislative session began on December 5th. Of the members meeting in the old House of Delegate chambers on the north side of the rotunda in the state capitol, 112 were newly elected and only 39 were returning to their second or more terms. Many important issues faced these men as they set about their work, chief among them the problem of certain banks issuing large quantities of worthless small denomination paper notes. Agriculture, free schools and

---

8.   *Ibid.*, Jones, "Forgotten Virginian," pp. 142-145.
9.   Horne Tooke, *Whose Overcoat Have You Got On?* (New York, 1854); "Virginia Calvacade," Spring 1970.

state finances were other pressing matters facing the legislators.[10]

Kemper was appointed to the House committees of propositions and grievances; courts of justice; banks; the special committee on the census; and the joint committee on the James River and Kanawha Canal Company. On December 8th, just three days after the opening of the session, Kemper introduced his first resolution. It called for the expediency of incorporating a turnpike company to build a road from Madison Mills to the Orange and Alexandria Railroad at Orange Court House.[11]

Kemper plunged into committee work and became more and more concerned with roads and transportation improvements.[12]

On December 10th, he introduced a second resolution to investigate the desirability of "adopting a more rigorous and efficient measure to prevent circulation of notes under five dollars."[13] On February 8, 1854, his plan became House Bill 351 and was debated in late February. It passed the House and was sent to the Senate where it was debated, passed with amendments and signed into public law.[14]

This was quite an accomplishment for a freshman legislator. While in Richmond, Kemper won respect and admiration of the people of Madison County by keeping them well informed of happenings and representing their best interests.

---

10.   Jones, "Forgotten Virginian," pp. 146-147.
11.   *Journal of the Virginia House of Delegates 1853-54* (hereafter referred to as House Journal) pp. 40-41.
12.   Jones, "Forgotten Virginian," pp. 156-157.
13.   House Journal, p. 61.
14.   *Ibid.*, pp. 283 and 404.

Chapter 6

The Coming Struggle

In 1855, Kemper was elected delegate to the Democratic Party's gubernatorial convention. The two top contenders for the party's nomination were Henry A. Wise and Shelton F. Leake. Since Leake was allied with George Nathaniel Thrift and Marcus Newman, Kemper threw all of his support behind Wise and worked vigorously in opposing Leake. Wise won the nomination and faced the Know-Nothing Party's candidate in the coming election, Thomas S. Flournoy of Halifax County, a former Whig. Wise beat Flournoy by 10,000 votes.[1] Kemper and Wise were to be strong supporters of one another for years to come.

Kemper had no opposition in the election of 1855 and was easily re-elected to the House of Delegates.[2]

Upon his return to the House, Kemper was appointed to three committees: courts of justice, library and militia laws. He was chosen as chairman of the latter. Three pressing issues faced the 1855-56 session of the General Assembly: internal improvements, banking and finance and the militia.[3] It was with his efforts to revitalize the militia that Kemper was to make his greatest impact in

---

1. Jones, "Forgotten Virginian," p. 162.
2. *Ibid.*, p. 165.
3. *Ibid.*, p. 167.

the future of Virginia and the South.

Since the Revolution, the state laws had called for each county to provide a company of militia with appropriate officers, and had required periodic drills and muster.[4] Changes to the law in 1851 and 1853 had abolished musters and discontinued the training of militia officers. Kemper opposed the changes, which, in effect, had done away with the militia, and sought to have them overturned.

On December 4, 1855, Kemper introduced a resolution to reform and reorganize the militia system, to restore musters and to provide for discipline and drill of the militia.[5] Kemper's resolution became House Bill 73, "To organize the militia and provide for the public defense of the Commonwealth."[6] There was considerable fight over the bill. The main argument against Kemper's proposal was the expense of implementing such a plan. By February, Kemper felt that he had enough support to go for a vote. The measure lost by ten votes, 70 to 60, but Kemper didn't give up. Public opinion was overwhelmingly in favor of the bill and the newspapers urged reconsideration. The House finally voted to reconsider and it passed 53 to 48 on March 4, 1856. There wasn't time for the Senate to consider the bill and it was carried over until the next session.[7]

Kemper's friendship with the adjutant-general of Virginia, William Richardson, blossomed as both believed in compulsory militia service and the organization of volunteer companies. Kemper's strong stance for the militia and intense devotion to states' rights and Southern rights increased his popularity dramatically throughout the state.

Richardson's high regard for Kemper is evidenced in this excerpt from a letter dated April 18, 1856: "It is notorious that you

---

4. "The History of the Militia in Madison County 1724-Present" by Sgt. Harold R. Woodward, Jr.
5. *House Journal 1855-56*, p. 50.
6. *Ibid.*, p. 131.
7. Jones, "Forgotten Virginian," pp. 176-177.

stood among the elite of the House of Delegates and in the very front rank and that although you consumed little of its time in debate, yet you were always to be found in your place and when you did speak it was always to the point, with fearless force and with effect."[8]

In 1856 Kemper was elected to the Democratic national convention held in Cincinnati, Ohio. Here he actively supported Governor Henry A. Wise for president. The convention was greatly split and finally in the seventeenth ballot, James Buchanan of Pennsylvania was nominated. Kemper campaigned actively for Buchanan in that year's election, and Buchanan was elected president of the United States.[9]

On May 13, 1856, Kemper was appointed to the board of visitors of Virginia Military Institute by Governor Wise for a term of two years. From the spring of 1857 to spring of 1858 he served as president of that board.[10]

Kemper faced no opposition in the election of 1857 and was elected to his third term in the House of Delegates. Again he was appointed to the courts of justice and militia laws committees. Kemper played a leading role in the 1857-58 session with his main interest being in the militia. The Senate passed his militia bill, which decreed that the governor was to appoint generals and field officers, and it became law. The plan was praised for being both effective and economical.[11] Kemper also pushed for an increase in salary for General Richardson.

Kemper managed to combine his roles of legislator, lawyer, husband and planter. Despite the low salary of a legislator, he was able to gain some wealth and provide a decent living for his fam-

---

8.   Kemper papers, U.Va.: letter from Adj. Gen. Richardson to Kemper April 18, 1856.
9.   *Ibid.*, pp. 180-185.
10.   *Ibid.*, p. 203.
11.   *Ibid.*, pp. 194-195.

ily; the majority of his income derived from his legal practice. He was a strong family man and regularly attended the Episcopal church with his wife. He and Belle enjoyed annual trips to one of Virginia's mineral springs for vacations and health reasons. During this period he received a voluminous amount of correspondence from all over the state, of both a political and non-political nature. It was also during this time that he acquired a taste for alcoholic drink.

Kemper was instrumental in the formation of the Lynn Banks Masonic Lodge. The lodge was named for Lynn Banks, long time state legislator, speaker of the House, and one of Madison County's most illustrious citizens. Kemper was named master of the lodge.[12]

In July 1858 Kemper was commissioned brigadier general of the First Brigade, Second Division of the Virginia Militia, upon promotion of his good friend General Robert Adam Banks. In his brigade were companies of men from the counties of Culpeper, Rappahannock, Madison, Orange, Greene, Spotsylvania and Caroline.[13]

Kemper was considered for lieutenant governor in 1858 and placed fourth in a field of six at the state convention. Kemper's old friend and college classmate John Letcher was the candidate for governor and R.L. Montague of Middlesex County was the candidate for lieutenant governor. Letcher was elected by 5,500 votes over his Whig opponent, W.L. Goggin of Bedford County. Once again Kemper faced no opposition in the race for the House of Delegates and in 1859 was sent to Richmond for his fourth term.[14]

In October of 1859 a madman named John Brown captured the federal arsenal at Harpers Ferry, intending to use the captured arms

---

12. *Ibid.*, pp. 201-202.
13. Lee A. Wallace, Jr. *A Guide to Virginia Military Organizations 1861-65* (Lynchburg, Virginia, 1986) p. 243; Jones, "Forgotten Virginian," p. 209.
14. Jones, "Forgotten Virginian," p. 210.

to equip slaves for a massive revolt against their white masters. Governor Wise ordered the militia and volunteer companies of the commonwealth to the scene. A company of United States Marines commanded by Colonel Robert E. Lee and Lieutenant James E. B. (Jeb) Stuart captured the deranged abolitionist and his accomplices, who were arrested and taken to Charles Town for trial. In November, following rumors of attempts to free the prisoners, more of the state's military forces were ordered out to stand guard duty. Included in this call up was the Richardson's Guards, Madison County's new volunteer company named in honor of Adjutant-General Richardson. The companies remained at Charles Town until December 2nd, when John Brown was hanged.[15]

Needless to say, Kemper was extremely proud of the Virginia militia and the role they played in bringing John Brown to justice. Both Governor Wise, in his last address to the General Assembly, and Governor Letcher, in his first address to that body, called for full-scale military preparedness. Governor Letcher praised the "gallant militia" for their effectiveness at Harpers Ferry and called for an appropriation of $50,000 to change outdated arms and provide for the "public defense." The legislature concerned itself with little more than John Brown, Harpers Ferry, and South Carolina's threat to secede from the Union if anti-southern activities continued.

In December, the name of Kemper's committee was changed from militia laws to military affairs.[16] Kemper introduced two bills, one calling for reorganization of the militia and the second for the purchase of arms and ammunition. Kemper's good friend John Barbour of Culpeper County introduced Bill Number 39 which called for $100,000 for purchase of arms. These and other bills relating to the militia were referred to the committee on military affairs.[17] As

---

15.   Woodward, "Militia."
16.   *House Journal 1859-60*, p. 39.
17.   Acts of the Virginia General Assembly 1859-60 (hereafter referred to as Acts of Assembly) p. 89.

chairman of this committee, Kemper was now one of the most powerful men in the state.

Out of this flurry of bills pertaining to the military came the Militia Act of March 30, 1860. This long, complex act spelled out many detailed refinements and important alterations in the militia system. It called for better organization and the formation of more volunteer companies including cavalry and artillery companies as well as light infantry. The bill called for drills six times a year for volunteer companies and twice a year for county militias. It required service of all able-bodied males between 18 and 45 years of age, and increased the fine for not attending musters. This bill also set forth the organization of volunteer companies into squadrons, battalions, and regiments and called for the state to provide arms for all volunteer companies.[18]

Kemper fought hard for this bill, and it passed 135 to 2. Other bills set the adjutant-general's salary at $2,000 annually (the governor increased it to $5,000) and provided additional funds for the Virginia Military Institute and the public guard. Kemper also supported "The Act Making an Appropriation for the Purchase and Manufacture of Arms and Munitions of War," an act designed to make the commonwealth of Virginia a self-sustaining military state. It set aside $180,000 for the purchase of weapons and provided nearly another $320,000 to build machinery and arsenals for the manufacture of weaponry and to patent newly invented armaments. Including all of the above, the state's military budget was in excess of $838,000, more than any other single budget item.[19]

As a result of Kemper's hard work and diligent pursuit of military reforms, Virginia was the best prepared of all southern states to face the coming struggle.

---

18.   *Ibid.*
19.   *Ibid., House Journal.*

Chapter 7

Secession

In the 1860 Presidential election, Kemper was a strong supporter of Henry A. Wise for president. The state Democratic convention was held in Charlottesville that year, and Kemper was delegated to represent Madison County. Thomas Jefferson Humphreys and General Robert Adam Banks were instrumental in getting Kemper selected for that position.[1]

Kemper also accompanied the Virginia delegation to the national convention in Baltimore that year. The Democratic Party was so split over sectional issues that they could not agree on a candidate to represent the party in the coming election. The debates were so heated that Senator William L. Yancey of South Carolina finally led the delegates from the deep South in walking out of the convention. Yancey, an ardent secessionist, urged the formation of a new party to advocate southern rights. The Virginia delegation also walked out of the convention; they did not, however, join Yancey and his followers. The remaining Democrats, those from the North and the West, finally nominated Senator Stephen Douglas of Illinois as their candidate.[2]

---

1.   Jones, "Forgotten Virginian," pp. 233-234.
2.   *Ibid.*, p. 235; Robert Selph Henry *The Story of the Confederacy* . (New York, 1931) p. 20.

The Southern Democrats met later in Charleston, South Carolina, and nominated John C. Breckenridge of Kentucky to represent their interests. Breckenridge, vice president under Buchanan, was a moderate who favored southern rights but opposed secession.

The states of the upper South—Virginia, Tennessee, Kentucky, and North Carolina—formed an opposition party. This new party, made up of remnants of the old-line Whig Party and the Know-Nothings, called themselves the Constitutional Union Party. They ran on a platform of "Union, the Constitution and the enforcement of the laws," and nominated John Bell of Tennessee for president.[3]

As the Democratic Party fell apart, a group with varied political views came together in Chicago; with their common bond of opposition to slavery, the new Republican Party nominated a virtually unknown lawyer from Illinois, Abraham Lincoln, as its candidate.[4]

Kemper supported Breckenridge because of his strong stance on states' rights. In the November election, Breckenridge carried all the states of the deep South; Bell carried Virginia, Kentucky, and Tennessee; Douglas carried only one southern state, Missouri. Lincoln swept every northern state but New Jersey, and although he received less than one-third of the popular vote, he secured enough electoral votes to be elected president.[5]

The election of Lincoln dashed all hopes that the federal government might sympathize with southern views, and a great alarm spread all across the South. The legislature of South Carolina called for a convention of the people to take action on the state's relationship with the federal government. They convened in Charleston on December 17th, and on the 20th, at noon, passed a brief ordinance declaring "that the Union now subsisting between South Carolina

---

3.   Henry, p. 21; Clement Eaton *A History of the Southern Confederacy* (New York, 1954) p. 2.

4.   *Ibid.*, p. 21.

5.   *Ibid.*, p. 21.

and other states, under the name of 'The United States of America' is hereby dissolved." The vote was unanimous.[6]

Mississippi followed South Carolina out of the Union on January 9th; Florida went out the next day, and Alabama the day after that. Georgia seceded on the 19th, and Louisiana joined them a week later. Representatives from these six states, at the suggestion of South Carolina and at the invitation of Alabama, met in Montgomery on February 4th to form a new confederation. On Saturday, February 9, 1861, Jefferson Davis of Mississippi and Alexander H. Stephens of Georgia were elected president and vice president of the provisional government of the Confederate States of America. Representatives from Texas joined the assembly in Montgomery, and there were then seven states in the new confederation.[7]

The Virginia legislature went into special session on January 7, 1861. At the urging of Governor Letcher, the legislators opted for a course of moderation. The General Assembly called for a Peace Convention, to meet in Washington, to work out a peaceful solution to the nation's problems. A former United States president, John Tyler of Virginia, chaired the convention, which included representatives from twenty-one states. Nothing came of these deliberations, and Tyler came away convinced that secession was Virginia's only alternative.[8]

At noon on the first day of the special session, Kemper, who thought it senseless for Virginia to remain in a hostile union, introduced a resolution calling for a committee of fifteen to support a bill to provide for a convention of the people to consider the state's course. He also urged military readiness on the state's part in case northern troops would try to cross Virginia in an effort to coerce the seceded states back into the Union. The vast majority of the members of the legislature supported Kemper and wanted Virginia to act

---

6.   *Ibid.*, p. 22.
7.   Henry, pp. 25-26.
8.   *Ibid.*, p. 26.

boldly and quickly and call a state convention.[9]

Kemper's resolution passed, and on January 8th he was chosen to head the committee. On the next day, he submitted a bill to call a convention and a proposal for election of members to the convention.[10] Richmond was in a great state of excitement. The population largely favored southern rights. There were large audiences at the meetings of the legislature and a number of great speeches were made on the floor. Kemper delivered a stirring speech on January 7th, in which he called for resistance against federal coercion.[11]

By January 10th, more than 140 public meetings held across the state had called for a state convention. When brought to a vote, Kemper's bill for election of delegates to the convention on February 2nd passed the House 141 to 0. It immediately went to the Senate, where it also passed by a great majority. The commonwealth's attorney, Angus R. Blakey, a good friend of Kemper's and a strong states' rights advocate, was elected to represent Madison County, which was overwhelmingly pro-Southern.[12]

Kemper stayed in Richmond during the convention, where he lent a great deal of weight and influence to the secessionists. In the legislature, Kemper was busy getting the state prepared militarily. An act of January 29, 1861, authorized $1,000,000 for the defense of the state and another $200,000 for coast, harbor and river defenses.[13] On March 14, 1861, an act passed calling for the issuance of $1,000,000 in treasury notes for use in defense of the state. Counties were authorized to borrow and issue bonds for the same purpose. The state also granted charters to three arms and munitions manufacturing companies. Kemper played a significant role in all of these

---

9.   Jones, "Forgotten Virginian," p. 239.
10.   *House Journal 1861-62*, pp. 3-4.
11.   *Ibid.*
12.   Jones, "Forgotten Virginian," p. 243.
13.   *Acts of Assembly 1861-62*, p. 28.

acts.[14]

Virginia began to buy military goods in the North and abroad. The state spent $10,000 for powder, $100,000 in camp equipment, and much more for shoes, buttons and uniforms from northern contractors, plus 500 pistols from the Colt Patented Firearms Company in Connecticut; 1,000 Enfield muskets from Great Britain; 3,000 sabres from Germany; and 296 cannon from various manufacturers.[15]

Kemper was re-appointed as a brigadier general in the Virginia militia on April 10th.[16]

In the seceded states, southern forces were capturing federal installations and garrisons. The last holdout was Fort Sumter in Charleston Harbor. A newly appointed brigadier-general in the Confederate States Army, Pierre Gustave Toutant Beauregard, was sent to command the forces gathering there and began immediately to fortify the harbor against possible reinforcements for the garrison from the sea. Negotiations for voluntary occupation were unsuccessful, and on April 11th the surrender of the fort was demanded. The major in charge of the fort's defense refused to surrender, and at 4:30 AM on April 12, 1861, the Confederate shore batteries began to bombard the fort. Throughout that day and the next night the bombardment continued. At 7:00 PM on the 13th, the fort finally surrendered.

Immediately following the fall of Fort Sumter, President Lincoln called for 75,000 troops to be supplied by the states for the purpose of putting down the rebellion.[17] Virginia was asked to supply 8,000

14.   *Ibid.*
15.   *Ibid.*
16.   "War of the Rebellion: A Compilation of the Official Records of the Union and Confederate Armies," (hereafter referred to as O.R.) (U.S. War Department, Washington, D.C., 1880-1891) Series 1, volume 51, p. 10: letter from Gov. John Letcher appointing and commissioning Kemper as brigadier general for the 1st Brig. Va. Forces dated April 10, 1861.
17.   Lamont Buchanan *A Pictorial History of the Confederacy* (New York, 1951) pp. 29-35.

of these troops.

Two days later, the convention passed the state's Ordinance of Secession by a vote of 88 to 55, to be voted on by the people at a special election in May. The day the ordinance passed, the legislature immediately authorized the governor to call into the service of the state as many volunteers that might be necessary to "repel invasion and protect the citizens of the state in the present emergency." On April 21st the governor called on volunteer companies to hold themselves in readiness for immediate orders. He appointed Robert E. Lee to command all the military and naval forces in Virginia, with the rank of major general, on April 23rd.[18] On the 24th, Virginia entered into a military alliance with the Confederacy.[19]

During this period Kemper received a tremendous volume of correspondence from all over the state, mostly concerning military affairs. His correspondents generally urged Virginia's support of the Confederacy.

Kemper's boyhood chum, Ambrose Powell Hill, requested a letter of support in his efforts to get a commission in the new Ordnance Department recently created by one of Kemper's bills. On April 22nd, Kemper recommended Hill to the governor, and Hill was soon commissioned as a colonel of volunteers.[20]

There was talk of Kemper campaigning for a seat in the Confederate Congress at Montgomery should Virginia join the Confederacy; however, military life appealed to Kemper more so than did politics. He was content with his commission as general and was active in the field, mainly raising troops and organizing companies. There was scarcely a county in the state without at least one volunteer company. Madison County had two.[21]

---

18. Wallace *Guide to Virginia Military Organizations* introduction.
19. Eaton, p. 53.
20. William Woods Hassler *A. P. Hill: Lee's Forgotten General* (Richmond, 1957) p. 28; Jones, "Forgotten Virginian," p. 269.
21. Jones, "Forgotten Virginian," pp. 270-272.

The military forces of Virginia were re-organized into three components: 1) the Provisional Army of Virginia, 2) the volunteers, and 3) the militia. The governor also reduced the number of general officers. Kemper was appointed colonel of volunteers on May 2nd, but was not assigned a unit command.

In late April and early May he attended a meeting in Alexandria with General Philip St. George Cocke, commander of the Potomac Department. Cocke was a good friend of Kemper's and they had served on the board of visitors at V.M.I. together. From the department headquarters in Culpeper, Kemper worked hard to organize the volunteers, especially those from Madison and surrounding counties. Once raised and organized, he set about arming the companies as best he could.

In mid-May, Kemper fell seriously ill. On May 23rd, while he was still away from his work, Virginians overwhelmingly approved the Ordinance of Secession, and shortly thereafter Virginia joined the Confederate States of America. The capital of the new nation was moved to Richmond from Montgomery.[22]

Kemper was back at work on June 1st and was given command of the newly-formed Seventh Virginia Regiment Volunteer Infantry.[23] On June 7th all of Virginia's forces were transferred to the Confederacy.[24] Kemper now began his long and illustrious career in the Provisional Army of the Confederate States.

---

22. *Ibid.*, p. 273.
23. O.R. ser 1, Vol. 51, p. 123: General Orders No. 24, June 1, 1861.
24. Jones, "Forgotten Virginian," p. 274.

Chapter 8

The Seventh Virginia Regiment

On June 1, 1861, the Seventh Virginia Regiment of Voluteers came into existence, and Kemper was appointed the commander.[1] Virginia's regiments were comprised of companies from neighboring counties when possible. Madison and the surrounding counties provided the majority of the Seventh Virginia's men, most of whom had enlisted between April and early June for terms of one year.

Madison County provided two companies to this regiment: A, known as Richardson's Guards, was under the command of Captain John Welch; and K, the Madison Grays, was commanded by Captain William Lovell. Neighboring Rappahannock County provided three companies: B, the Washington Grays, under Captain Thomas B. Massie; G, the Rappahannock Guard, under Captain Austin J. Walden; and the Sperryville Sharpshooters under Captain J. Catlett Gibson. The Sharpshooters received no alphabetical designation and only served with the regiment until early August, when they transferred to the Forty-ninth Virginia.[2]

---

1.   O.R. Series 1, vol. 51, p. 123.
2.   Louis Ford Hitt, "The 7th Virginia Infantry Regiment, C.S.A." (V.P.I. & S.U. Master Thesis, 1972) pp. 2-5; David Riggs *7th Virginia Infantry* (Lynchburg, Virginia, 1985) pp. 1-2; David E. Johnson *The Story of a Confederate Boy in the Civil War* (Portland, Oregon, 1914) pp. 54-55.

Culpeper County supplied the regiment with two companies: C under Captain John C. Porter and E, the Hazlewood Volunteers, under Captain John Taylor. Company C also contained a considerable number of men from Orange County, and Captain Porter was soon replaced by Captain J.W. Almond of Orange County. Company F from Greene County, commanded by Captain Francis Marion McMullen, and Company I, the Holcombe Guards under Captain John J. Winn, were the other companies from the same geographical area.[3]

The regiment's remaining two companies came from considerable distances away. Company H, the Washington Volunteers from Washington, D.C., under Captain William Cleary, and Company D, the Mountain Boomers from Giles County in southwest Virginia, were latecomers to the regiment.[4]

The Richardson's Guards mustered on April 28th and were immediately ordered to Alexandria. They marched twenty miles to Gordonsville, where they boarded the cars of the Virginia Central Railroad. After a few days they returned to Madison, then marched twenty-three miles to Culpeper and mustered into the Confederate army. They were one of the better-equipped companies in the army, with modern Springfield muskets and good uniforms provided by the people of Madison County.[5] Colonel Kemper remarked that they were "in a good state of discipline and drill." They joined the rest of the Seventh Virginia on June 30th[6] at Camp Wigfall, a grassy area southeast of Manassas Junction, where the new recruits were to learn the fundamentals of army life.[7]

---

3.   *Ibid.*
4.   *Ibid.*
5.   Taxes were raised to provide for this company; Harold R. Woodward, Jr. *For Home and Honor: The Story of Madison County Virginia During the War Between the States, 1861-65* (Madison, Virginia, 1990) p. 21.
6.   Hitt, p. 2.
7.   Riggs, p. 1. (The camp was named for General Louis T. Wigfall of

The rest of the companies were not so well prepared. Company K, raised on April 23rd by James W. Twyman, was inferior in both drill and discipline, with inadequate clothing and no accoutrements. They were armed with old flintlock muskets recently altered to percussion, which were of very poor quality.[8] By June 30th, Kemper was able to report that "their drill and discipline is improving."[9]

Captain Massie's Company B reported with one uniform and one altered musket per man and lacked any experience at drilling. The Hazlewood Volunteers, on the other hand, were well trained and drilled but armed with flintlock muskets; each man was uniformed in a black shirt and gray pants. Company I was well attired in handsome gray uniforms made by the ladies of Albemarle County.[10]

The men of Company H were refugees from the District of Columbia and Maryland. They were completely without uniforms and accoutrements, and since their personal effects were now in enemy territory, they could only turn to the Confederate government for supplies. Although armed only with old flintlock muskets, the company was well trained and disciplined, "its one shining asset," noted Kemper.[11]

Company D had originally been assigned to the Twenty-fourth Virginia, but a quarrel between Lieutenant Eustace Gibson of the company and Lieutenant Colonel George Hairston, the regiment's second-in-command, had caused such intense hostility that they were transferred to Kemper's regiment.[12]

South Carolina, who had demanded the surrender of Fort Sumter from Maj. Robert Anderson.)

8.   Woodward, *For Home and Honor*, p. 22; Riggs, p. 3; Hitt, p. 3.
9.   Hitt, p. 3.
10.   *Ibid.*, pp. 5-6.
11.   *Ibid.*, p. 4.
12.   Johnson, p. 53; Riggs, p. 1.

The Seventh Virginia was a young regiment, predominantly farm boys under the age of twenty-two. At Camp Wigfall they learned the basics of soldiering, enduring long hours of drilling and adjusting to the rigors of life in the infantry. The undisciplined troops spent hours on picket duty where anything that moved in the direction of the enemy was apt to be shot at. After many false alarms, they weren't allowed to have cartridges.[13] Another problem that soon remedied itself was the troops' inexperience at cooking. At first they put everything they had into a large pot and boiled it, but the inedible results compelled them to learn how to cook.[14]

Kemper's staff consisted of Lieutenant-Colonel Lewis B. Williams of Orange County, Major Waller Tazewell Patton of Culpeper County, Dr. C.B. Morton as surgeon, the reverends John H. Bocock (Kemper's brother-in-law) and Florence M. McCarthey as chaplains, Captain Nelson Crisler as quartermaster, and Captain J.W. Green as commissary. Charles C. Floweree was the adjutant, and George S. Tansill was the sergeant-major.

As these men attended to the needs of their troops and taught them the fundamentals, General Beauregard was structuring his regiments into an army. On June 20th, the Seventh Virginia was assigned to the brigade of Colonel Jubal A. Early,[15] which included the Seventh Louisiana under Colonel Henry T. Hays of Tennessee (recently transplanted to Louisiana) and the Twenty-Fourth Virginia under Colonel William R. Terry.[16]

Early in July, Kemper was detached from his regiment to serve as quartermaster for General Beauregard at Fairfax Court House. When the union army began to advance, it was Kemper's responsibility to move the baggage and supply wagons behind Mitchell's

---

13.   Hitt, p. 10.
14.   Johnson, p. 44.
15.   *Ibid.*, pp. 54-55; Riggs, p. 2.
16.   Hitt, p. 13.

Ford on Bull Run near Manassas.[17]

General Beauregard praised Kemper for his handling of this duty in his report to Adjutant-General Samuel Cooper in Richmond: "It is due, however, to Col. J.L. Kemper, Va. Forces, to express my sense of the value of his services in the preparation for and execution of the retreat from Fairfax C.H. on Bull Run. Called from the head of his regiment, by what appeared to me an imperative need of the service, to take charge of the superior duties of the Quartermaster Department with the advance at the critical juncture, he accepted the responsibilities involved, and was eminently successful."[18]

General M.L. Bonham also praised Kemper's service as quartermaster, referring to Kemper's "activity and efficiency" in his report.[19]

---

17. Jones, "Forgotten Virginian," p. 275.
18. *Ibid.*, p. 275; O.R. Ser. 1, vol. II, pp. 440-450.
19. O.R. Ser. 1, vol. II, pp. 449-459.

Chapter 9

First Taste of Battle

Early's brigade, strengthened by the Thirteenth Mississippi and three cannon from the Washington Artillery of Louisiana, marched to Camp Walker on Bull Run at McLean's Ford on Wednesday, July 17th. The Seventh Virginia, under the command of Lieutenant Colonel Williams, was posted at the front gate of the McLean farm,[1] their rations now cut to one meal per day.[2]

Early the next morning the brigade moved a short distance to an eminence overlooking Mitchell's, Blackburn's and McLean's fords. About noon they observed clouds of dust to the north and heard the rattle of musketry as a brisk skirmish began, followed by the roar of cannon from the direction of Mitchell's Ford.[3] The federal troops of Colonel Israel B. Richardson's brigade were approaching Blackburn's Ford at a bend in Bull Run between Mitchell's Ford to the west and McLean's Ford to the southeast.

The Seventh Virginia passed General Beauregard on their way to join the fray. Beauregard urged his men on, saying, "Keep cool, men, and fire low." General James Longstreet, whose brigade was engaged with Richardson's brigade, appealed to Early for rein-

---

1.   Hitt, p. 13.
2.   Letter of George Mason Bohannon quoted in Woodward, p. 45.
3.   Johnson, p. 63.

forcements. Beauregard replied by ordering "Old Jube" to send two regiments and two guns. He complied by sending the Seventh Virginia and the Seventh Louisiana. The untested troops neared the front, sobered by the sight of casualties from the First Virginia. As they advanced along a narrow country lane at the double quick, they broke into a wild and menacing rebel yell, the first time this soon-to-be-famous sound was heard.[4]

The Seventh Virginia received their baptismal fire as they emerged into an open field two hundred yards from Bull Run. Charging into battle, they were met with a hail of fire from the Yankees. The marksmanship of the northern soldiers was poor, however, and most of the shots went high. The regiment relieved Longstreet's First Virginia at the bank of the stream. The enemy was pushed back, but an artillery duel continued until dark. The engagement at Blackburn's Ford was over; the Seventh Virginia had had its first taste of battle, and seven of its number had fallen wounded.[5]

Kemper rejoined his unit on the 18th and was warmly welcomed by his men. Lieutenant Colonel Williams was a strict disciplinarian who punished even minor infractions, and the men were glad to have Kemper back in command.

The weary soldiers awoke at daylight, having lain on their arms all night. They gathered up quite a number of muskets, knapsacks, blankets, canteens and cartridge boxes thrown down during the previous day's fighting by the enemy. They spent the rest of that day and all of the next constructing breastworks and preparing for another attack. The regiment remained at Blackburn's Ford until Saturday evening, when it was relieved and returned to the pine thicket near the McLean farm.[6]

Kemper's regiment at that time numbered less than four hundred

---

4.   Johnson, p. 65.
5.   Riggs, p. 3.
6.   *Ibid.*, p. 3.

men, primarily due to illness.[7] The inexperienced fighters had done well in their first engagement, and their colonel was understandably proud of their performance. They felt ready for the coming battle that many on both sides believed could end the war.

At sunrise on Sunday, July 21st, Kemper and his men were awakened by the enemy's batteries near Blackburn's Ford. The Seventh Virginia and Seventh Louisiana waited in the pines in support of Longstreet's and Brigadier General David R. Jones's brigades, on the extreme right of the Confederate line. The enemy gunners occasionally managed to drop a shell into their protected position, scattering dirt and dust, but did no serious damage.[8]

While preparing to reinforce Jones's brigade, Early was ordered to cross Bull Run at Blackburn's Ford and silence the union batteries there. Upon reaching their intended position, Early was ordered to bring his brigade at once to the extreme left of the Confederate line, nearly eight miles away. The day was sweltering, without a hint of breeze during the forced march. They arrived at General Joseph E. Johnston's headquarters around 1:00 PM.[9]

Early marched to the rear of Mitchell's Ford, toward the firing near the stone bridge. He had under his immediate command Kemper's Seventh Virginia, Hays's Seventh Louisiana and Colonel William Barksdale's Thirteenth Mississippi. From Johnston they learned that Beauregard wanted all reinforcements with him at the front. Johnston directed Early to strike at the union right. The Mississippians and Louisianans formed on the left of the Seventh Virginia, overlapping the union line and causing some momentary confusion. Early's brigade formed on the left of Brigadier General Arnold Elzey's brigade and, almost simultaneously, Lieutentant Colonel J.E.B. Stuart's cavalry formed on Early's left. Early paused briefly to confirm the identity of the troops opposite them on Bald

---

7.   *Ibid.*, pp. 3-4.
8.   Johnson, p. 73; Hitt, p. 18; Jones, p. 277.
9.   Hitt, p. 18; Jones, p. 277.

Hill, then the Confederate line surged forward. It was nearly 4:00 PM.[10]

A single volley from the Confederate muskets sent the northerners into retreat. With a thundering rebel yell, the whole Confederate force advanced. General Beauregard ordered a general pursuit, and Early's brigade, reinforced by Colonel Philip St. George Cocke with one regiment, continued on past the Matthews, Drogan and Carter houses. One mile above the Stone Bridge, the exhausted troops halted for the night. The Seventh Virginia had lost nine killed and thirty-eight wounded, the heaviest losses in the brigade. The next day the pursuit continued as far as Centreville, where the Seventh Virginia rested for several days.[11]

The Confederates were amazed at the amount of plunder left behind by the retreating Yankees. The roads to Washington were littered with discarded spoils of every sort. Hundreds of horses, wagons, cannons, harness, spades, shovels, picks, axes, clothes, knapsacks, blankets, medicines and even handcuffs were recovered. They had a field day gathering up items left behind by the fleeing northerners. The food, wine and champagne were put to good use. Several men got money, watches and other valuables from the dead Yankees. Even Colonel Kemper took seven hundred and twenty dollars from one Yankee's pockets.[12]

Kemper's ability as quartermaster was once again put to the test by Beauregard, who planned to pursue the Yankees all the way to Washington and end the war. Kemper was ordered to obtain enough wagons and teams to allow the army to accomplish that mission. In all he procured two hundred wagons,[13] including forty

---

10.   Riggs, p. 4; Hitt, p. 19; Johnson, pp. 73-74.
11.   Riggs, p. 4; Hitt, pp. 20-21.
12.   Bohannon Letter, Woodward, pp. 46-49.
13.   Jed Hotchkiss, ed. by General Clement A. Evans *Confederate Military History: Extended Edition, Vol. IV, Virginia* (Wilmington, N.C., 1987), p. 620.

wagons and teams that Captain Crisler brought from Madison County.[14]

Kemper was praised by many for his performance at Manassas. Early reported that Kemper "displayed great coolness and gallantry in front of his regiment while they were being formed under a galling fire from the enemy's sharpshooters."[15] H.N. Wallace of Madison complimented Kemper in a letter, remarking, "And now Colonel, will you permit me with heartfelt pride to congratulate you on your great gallantry in the late terrible battle."[16] "Congratulations upon flattering accounts of bearing and conduct as a soldier and an officer," wrote Delegate B.H. Wayland of Albemarle County.[17]

Kemper's old friend, Adjutant General William Richardson wrote:

> You have faithfully and nobly served our dear Old Mother Virginia in her halls of council and periled your life in defense of her sovereignty and her rights in the field. . . . I know you did your duty and gallantly too—and *I am* thankful that you were there. . . . [I]t was gallantly and nobly done, all of it, and proves the invincibility of Southern men.[18]

Four days after the battle, on July 25th, Beauregard reorganized his army; brigades were now set up by states. The Seventh Virginia was assigned to Longstreet's brigade, along with the First, Eleventh, and Seventeenth Virginia.[19] Now known as the Fourth Brigade, they would see much action together in the coming years.

---

14.   Woodward, p. 47.
15.   O.R. Ser. 1, vol. II, p. 555.
16.   Kemper papers, U. Va., letter from H.N. Wallace, July 27, 1861.
17.   *Ibid.*, letter from B.H. Wayland, August 26, 1861.
18.   *Ibid.*, letter from W.H. Richardson, August 1, 1861.
19.   Riggs, p. 5; Hitt, p. 21.

Chapter 10

Grim Reality

Beauregard's long-awaited pursuit of the retreating Yankee army never happened, and the South realized that this would not be the short, quick war everyone had hoped for. The battle of Manassas was a Confederate victory, but the southern leaders acknowledged the need for more and better troop training if they were to fight a successful war. Kemper's ability in this area was recognized by many as previously noted.

His contribution to the southern victory, however, was greater than even his champions realized. Forty-three of the forty-seven cannon the Confederate army had on the field at Manassas belonged to the commonwealth of Virginia, the material result of Kemper's legislative efforts to strengthen the militia. The credit for Virginia's military preparedness should go solely to the far-sighted patriot from Madison County.

The Seventh Virginia spent the next few weeks east of Centreville, then moved closer to Fairfax Court House.[1] The men settled into the camp routine, performed picket duty, and looked for packages from home. Colonel Kemper's family sent him food, clothing, and other items by way of his trusted servant Sam.[2]

---

1.   Riggs, p. 5.
2.   Jones, p. 280.

In August, while on picket duty, the Seventh Virginia spotted a Yankee observation balloon from Munson's Hill,[3] and on August 29th, the regiment engaged in a skirmish there.[4] Captain Lovell of Company K led his men and those of Company D in this sharp fight. The next day, Saturday, August 30th, Major Patton, leading Companies B and D, advanced to Bailey's Crossroads, where they saw action against the Second Michigan. In both instances the enemy was repulsed, with one lieutenant of Company B slightly wounded as the only casualty in the regiment.[5]

In a few days the regiment returned to camp. The weather was extremely hot and dry, the drinking water was bad, and the men were generally inactive. Disease took its toll in numbers but the ranks were bolstered by some new recruits. Other than some company drill, picket duty and quarter guard, they did little but eat, sleep and write letters for several weeks.[6]

On October 15th, Beauregard moved his army from Fairfax Court House to winter quarters at Centreville. During the move, Kemper's regiment lost most of its tents in a fire. In November the men built log huts with wood and clay chimneys for their winter shelters. Summer's heat was replaced by winter—long, cold and even more dreary because of the scarcity of rations. It was difficult to get supplies over the rutted, muddy roads.[7]

Boredom, disease, military bureaucracy and lice (called graybacks by the troops) were constant companions. The one event that created excitement that winter was the unveiling of a new battle flag for the army. Most of the Confederate regiments carried their state flags, many of which were difficult to distinguish from flags carried by the enemy. Even more confusing was the Confederate First Na-

---

3.   Hitt, p. 22.
4.   Hitt, p. 21
5.   Johnson, p. 77; Hitt, p. 22.
6.   *Ibid.*, p. 78.
7.   *Ibid.*, p. 81; Riggs, p. 5.

tional banner, which when furled was hard to tell apart from the United States flag.

General Beauregard finally designed a new flag, one that was only to be carried into battle. After conferring with Johnston and others, he settled on a red field crossed by diagonal blue bars on which were white stars. The War Department approved the design, and solemn ceremonies, followed by great banquets and celebrations, were held in honor of the new symbol of the Confederate army.[8]

Many terms of enlistment were due to expire soon, but the introduction of a fifty-dollar bounty and thirty-day furlough prompted re-enlistments. General Longstreet was promoted to division command; Brigadier General Richard Ewell now led the brigade. There was little interest among the men over these changes, but there was great anxiety over Kemper's absence from the regiment while attending to his legislative duties when the General Assembly was in session, primarily because of Lieutenant Colonel Williams reputation as a strict disciplinarian.[9]

Kemper's involvement in politics grew. Some of his friends and allies supported him for election to the Confederate Senate. Others supported him for speaker of Virginia's House of Delegates. On December 2nd, Kemper was nominated for speaker by his friend John Barbour and was elected without opposition. He had an excellent record of attendance during the session despite frequent bouts of ill health. He voted on nearly every measure, including twenty-five of a military nature.[10]

Kemper favored a system of appointment and promotion for company and regimental officers rather than the election of officers that was then in effect. Generals A.P. Hill and Jubal Early also fa-

8.   T. Harry Williams *P.G.T. Beauregard: Napoleon in Gray* (Baton Rouge, 1955) pp. 109-110.
9.   Riggs, p. 6.
10.   Jones, pp. 283-285.

vored appointment over election, but despite Kemper's efforts and their support, the election of officers continued.[11]

During the winter, long-standing differences between General Beauregard and President Davis worsened. The nation was split between pro-Beauregard or anti-administration factions and those supporting the president. Congressmen, governors and generals took sides in the dispute. Beauregard had the support of several former aides who were now in the Confederate Congress: William P. Miles, James R. Chestnut and Roger A. Pryor. He sought Kemper's support; as speaker of the House of Delegates, Kemper was one of the most influential men in the state. Kemper supported his former commander, but didn't get too deeply involved in the uproar.[12]

Although he was busy with political matters, Kemper was kept informed of military affairs while he was in Richmond. On February 28, 1862, he received a report from a Colonel Dimmock on the state of the defenses of Richmond.[13]

In early March, he requested a leave from the General Assembly to rejoin his regiment, and on the 25th the House unanimously issued a resolution expressing its thanks to Kemper for "the able, impartial, and dignified manner in which he has discharged the duties imposed upon him," and offered, "good wishes . . . for future happiness and success."[14]

Kemper's regiment had moved out of winter camp on March 8th and were poised to face union General George B. McClellan's force on the Virginia peninsula, between the York and the James rivers, when he rejoined them.

The army had been reorganized, and General Johnston was now in command. The Seventh Virginia was assigned to A.P. Hill's

---

11.   *Ibid.*, p. 285.
12.   Williams, p. 112.
13.   O.R. Ser. 1, vol. 51, p. 46.
14.   House Journal 1861-62, p. 311.

brigade.[15] Ewell was transferred to the Valley and the troops commanded by General Thomas J. Jackson. On April 26th, Kemper was re-elected to command the Seventh Virginia. Waller T. Patton was elected lieutenant-colonel, and Charles C. Floweree was elected major.[16]

On April 29th, the troops filed into the trenches built under the supervision of General John B. Magruder near Yorktown.[17] They were vastly outnumbered, however, and the Confederates soon withdrew from Yorktown toward Richmond. Marching through the knee-deep mud, Kemper's regiment retreated to Lebanon Church, near Williamsburg, on May 3rd.[18]

Here the army was poised for the coming battle. General Hill wrote that Kemper possessed, "that military quickness and intuition that prove the thorough soldier."[19] An adequate description indeed.

---

15.   O.R. Ser. 1, vol. 9, p. 41.
16.   *Ibid.*, p. 32.
17.   Hitt, p. 32.
18.   *Ibid.*, p. 34.
19.   Jones, p. 289.

Chapter 11

The Peninsula Campaign

Kemper's regiment took position in front of the Eastern Hospital for the Insane at Williamsburg. The enemy had followed their retreat closely, skirmishing briskly with the rear guard. The next day was spent standing in line of battle from early dawn until nearly noon, listening the distant rattle of musketry and the boom of artillery. Hill's brigade then advanced down the road past the College of William and Mary. Crossing open fields raked by artillery fire, they moved in support of Brigadier General Cadmus M. Wilcox's troops. Wilcox attacked the Federals with Hill close behind. Kemper's men rushed forward with a rebel yell. The Yankees fell back and the Seventh Virginia took a position forty-five yards from their enemy, behind a rail fence. On their left was the Seventeenth Virginia; the Eleventh Virginia was on their right.[1]

Soon a new union force formed opposite Hill's brigade. After assessing the situation, Hill ordered Kemper forward. The Seventh Virginia hurled an all-out assault at an opportune moment and, with the Eleventh and Seventeenth Virginia, pushed back the stubborn Yankees. Upon reaching a field of fallen timber, the Virginians took cover behind the logs. Musket fire continued for over two

---

1. Riggs, p. 7; Hitt, p. 35.

hours. With ammunition running low, Hill ordered a bayonet charge. The Federals fled in the face of this renewed attack, with the First Virginia and Nineteenth Mississippi joining in the pursuit.[2]

The Seventh Virginia fell back to reorganize and refill their cartridge boxes from those of their dead enemy.[3] The Federals had lost eight pieces of artillery and one flag to the Virginians. Around 5:00 PM Brigadier General Raleigh Colston's brigade moved in to relieve Hill's troops. At 7:00 PM Hill received orders to withdraw.[4]

Hill's report on the battle of Williamsburg heaped praise on Kemper and his men. He noted that they had "dashed in with a cheer," during the first charge. In the second charge, Hill reported, "their gallant colonel led his men as they bounded over the fence."[5] General Longstreet mentioned Kemper's "marked skill and fearlessness" in his report of the battle.[6] Lieutenant Colonel Patton and Major Floweree also were cited for gallantry in the battle.[7] Private Mays, the color bearer of the Seventh Virginia, received praise for having the flagstaff shot from his grasp twice; the colors suffered twenty-seven bullet holes. In all the regiment lost thirteen killed in action and sixty-four wounded in the battle.[8]

Despite fatigue and hunger, the Confederates marched in good spirits. Two of the men in Company D, spotting an elderly preacher with white hair and long white beard, shouted, "Boys, here is old Father Abraham." The old minister retorted, "Young man, you are mistaken. I am Saul, the son of Kish, searching for his father's

---

2.   *Ibid.*, p. 7; Hitt, pp. 36-37; Martin Schenck *Up Came Hill: The Story of the Light Division and its Leaders* (Harrisburg, Pennsylvania, 1958) p. 73.
3.   O.R. Ser. 1, vol. 9, pt. 1, p. 577.
4.   Riggs, p. 7.
5.   Hitt, p. 36.
6.   O.R. Ser. 1, vol. 9, pt. 1, p. 567.
7.   Hitt, p. 37.
8.   *Ibid.*, p. 37.

asses, and I have found them."[9]

On May 9th, the Seventh Virginia crossed the Chickahominy River and bivouacked at Clark's farm. By the 17th, they were at Howard's Grove on higher, dryer ground with better water. The sultry weather was spent in camp, except for May 22nd-23rd when the regiment was on picket duty. On the night of May 30th there was a violent thunderstorm accompanied by a downpour of rain which flooded the camp, forcing the men to stand the rest of the night. At daylight on May 31st, the order came to march.[10]

Once in the vicinity of Seven Pines, Kemper's men were held in reserve near the Williamsburg Road. The fighting began around 1:00 PM. General Johnston led his army in an attack on McClellan's IV Corps under Major General Erasmus Keys. Hill had been promoted to division commander, and Kemper was now acting brigade commander. The Seventh was led by Waller Patton.[11]

At 4:00 PM General G.W. Smith's division was engaged in desperate combat with General Silas Casey's federal division. The Seventh Virginia was about three-fourths of a mile from the federal lines, to the right of the road leading toward Seven Pines, when Kemper was ordered to attack in support of Smith.[12]

He ordered his brigade into the woods at the double quick, the Seventh Virginia in the van, where they encountered many wounded men leaving the battle area. They continued their advance under increasingly heavy artillery fire.[13]

As Kemper led his men farther into the miry brush, the smoke of battle obscured their surroundings, smoke so thick that Kemper could not distinguish his separate regiments,[14] smoke so thick that

9.   Riggs, p. 7.
10.   Johnson, pp. 103-104.
11.   Riggs, p. 8.
12.   Hitt, p. 39.
13.   *Ibid.*, p. 39.
14.   Clifford Dowdey *The Seven Days: The Emergence of Lee* (Boston,

they blundered into the federal camp, where there erupted a tremendous fire that ripped through the ranks. Many of Kemper's men were killed or wounded, and his troops fled back to the entrenchments, little more than muddy ditches, at the edge of the camp. From here they exchanged shots with the enemy for the next two hours.[15] Despite their predicament, Kemper organized a flank attack, which cleared the woods of enemy troops and saved the day.[16]

The brigade held the captured ground until 9:00 PM, then withdrew to the rear, where they bivouacked. Many of them searched for their missing comrades and enemy booty, especially heavily-laden union knapsacks.[17] The brigade remained in position until relieved at noon the following day and returned to camp on June 2. One significant result of the battle of Seven Pines was the unfortunate wounding of General Johnston, who was replaced by General Robert E. Lee.[18]

Kemper's performance at the battle of Seven Pines was recognized by his superiors. General Johnston called particular attention to the fact that he had led a command above his grade.[19] General Longstreet noted Kemper's "usual gallantry and ability" and his "spirit and regularity."[20] General Lee recognized Kemper's ability and wrote President Davis on June 2nd, asking for the immediate appointment of Kemper to brigadier general.[21] President Davis replied by making the appointment that very day.[22] This quick advancement was extremely unusual in the Confederate army and

1964) p. 99.

15. Hitt, p. 40.
16. *Ibid.*, p. 40.
17. *Ibid.*, p. 40.
18. Riggs, p. 8.
19. O.R. Ser. 1, vol. 9, pt. 1, p. 935.
20. *Ibid.*, pp. 939-940.
21. Douglas Southall Freeman I (New York, 1942) vol. 1, p. 267.
22. O.R. Ser. 1, vol. XI, pt. 2, p. 569.

was the equivalent to a field promotion for valor.

One anonymous description of Kemper at the battle of Seven Pines, widely quoted in the newspapers, illustrates his penchant for getting into the thick of combat with his men: "[H]is bright, new uniform bedaubed with mud, [he was] in the trenches, in the mud, and water."

On June 4th the brigade reached camp midway between Richmond and the Seven Pines battlefield, to the south of the Williamsburg Road. The two weeks in camp were spent drilling, undergoing inspections, and enduring more heavy rain with no protection from the downpours. On the 18th there was heavy skirmishing. On the 27th the brigade marched out toward Mechanicsville.[23]

While encamped near Darbytown on the Mechanicsville Turnpike, Kemper was formally placed in command of the brigade he had in fact commanded for nearly a month. The First Virginia was then commanded by Colonel Frederick G. Skinner; the Seventh by Colonel Patton; the Eleventh by Colonel David Funsten; the Seventeenth by Colonel Montgomery D. Corse; and the Twenty-fourth by Colonel William R. Terry. The Twenty-fourth had just recently joined the brigade, having been transferred from the command of Brigadier General Samuel Garland.[24]

Sergeant Charles T. Loehr of the First Virginia described the extraordinary comeraderie among the men of Kemper's brigade:

[T]he men of this old brigade came to know and love each other. Standing together, shoulder to shoulder, facing the storm of lead and iron on so many battlefields, traveling together so many weary miles, from the swamps of North Carolina to the

23. Hitt, pp. 42-44.
24. Virginia Regimental History Series by H. E. Howard Co., Lynchburg, Virginia, volumes on 1st, 7th, 11th, 17th and 24th Virginia Regiments; Charles T. Loehr *War History of the Old First Virginia Infantry Regiment, Army of Northern Virginia* (Richmond, 1884).

Mountains of Pennsylvania, made them comrades and brothers indeed. Never, to my knowledge, was there the slightest discord or strife between the various regiments composing this brigade. An insult to a member of this brigade was an insult to be resented by every individual man of the brigade. Right or wrong, they would assist and stand by each other; one relying on the other with implicit faith—these were "Kemper's Men."[25]

Hereafter designated the First Brigade of Longstreet's Division, Kemper's brigade would become one of the most distinguished in the Army of Northern Virginia. When Kemper took command, he had his old regiment, the Seventh Virginia, formed. Mounted on his horse before of the ranks, he spoke with patriotic fervor, eulogizing the men for their courage and devotion to the cause and expressing his love and devotion to them all, declaring that, "Next to the child that sprang from my own loins, I love the Seventh Regiment."[26]

General Kemper delivered another "soul-stirring speech," the evening his brigade broke camp:[27]

Soldiers, the great battle of the Revolution is now about to be fought; if we are successful the Confederacy is a free country and we will go home together; if we are beaten the war must go on for years. The bayonet is the chief implement to be relied on. You may stand at the distance of three or four hundred yards and fire all day at the enemy and they won't run, but when the point of your bayonets comes to glisten at their bosoms they won't stand. Keep well your places in ranks and preserve your organization.

---

25. Loehr, p. 23.
26. W. H. Morgan *Personal Reminiscences of the War of 1861-65* (Lynchburg, Virginia, 1911) p. 115.
27. Ralph White Gunn *24th Virginia Infantry* (Lynchburg, Virginia, 1987) p. 27.

Before dawn the troops formed ranks and hurried toward the sound of battle, marching about an hour before being halted. They broke ranks and spread out on both sides of the road, where they ate and relaxed, then crossed the Chickahominy River at Meadow Bridge. While marching toward the previous day's battlefield at Mechanicsville, they got their first glimpse of General Lee and his famous horse, Traveler. About mid-day they reached Mechanicsville and there witnessed the ruins of the battle.

The little hamlet had been reduced to a heap of debris. Bodies shredded by the canister shot of the cannons lay on the ground, still unburied. Horses, wagons and military equipment of every description were scattered about. After an hour at Mechanicsville, the brigade moved out to the southeast, in the direction of the firing at Gaines's Mill.[28]

Although held in reserve at the battle of Gaines's Mill, the First Brigade was often well within range of the enemy's artillery. While the brigade rested in a woods just north of the battle, A.P. Hill's division was in a desperate struggle with the union forces. The Virginians had just begun to feast on bacon and coffee, compliments of the enemy, when skirmishing broke out. They quickly gathered their arms and sprang to action under sporadic rifle fire. At sundown they advanced at the double quick toward the sound of battle. Upon reaching Gaines's Mill, the men had to watch their step, as the ground was literally covered with wounded men.

The Virginians climbed a small hill and halted behind a series of breastworks that had been acquired at heavy cost by the Texans of General John Bell Hood's command. Below the hill, other Confederate units were still engaged. The First Brigade was ordered to "charge bayonets!" Advancing down the hill at a dead run, they met the enemy. Only a single volley was fired, and McClellan's army

---

28.   *Ibid.*, p. 27.

turned in full retreat. The Confederate forces had won the day.[29]

The night of the 28th of June was spent sorting through the spoils left behind by the Yankees. The Virginians outfitted themselves with new clothing, knapsacks and blankets. Many of the men traded their smoothbore muskets for Enfield rifles.

The morning of June 29th, Kemper's brigade crossed the Chickahominy River on an abandoned Yankee pontoon bridge, a new experience for them. From the river at New Bridge they headed due south, reached the Darbytown Road, then proceeded eastward. All through the day and most of the night, the men endured one of the hardest marches of the war, battling heat, humidity, a lack of drinking water and the suffocating dust created by the constant tramping of thousands of weary feet. Only by abandoning the road for the fields could they find fresh air. The urgency of their mission forbade any rest stops, and heat stroke and exhaustion took their toll. The brigade finally halted near midnight, and the men fell fast asleep without even a mouthful of food.[30]

June 30th dawned bright and clear. Up at daylight, the men hurriedly downed a simple breakfast and resumed their march. The pace was more relaxed, and there were ample stops for rest. At mid-morning the column left the Darbytown Road and headed down the Long Bridge Road. At 3:00 PM they halted and formed a line of battle to the right of the Charles City Road, which led toward Frayser's farm.

Longstreet's Division was on the right of the Confederate line, with the First Brigade was on the extreme right of the division. The regiments were deployed from left to right in this order: the Twenty-fourth, the Seventh, the First and the Eleventh, with the Seventeenth protecting the flank. Skirmishers were sent out, and they came under heavy fire.[31]

At 5:00 PM they received the order to attack. According to Gen-

29.   *Ibid.*, pp. 27-28.
30.   *Ibid.*, pp. 28-29.
31.   *Ibid.*, p. 29; Hitt, p. 44.

eral E. Porter Alexander, Longstreet's chief of artillery, "The order to move forward and attack was first received by Kemper's brigade, which held the right flank in the dense woods with its right regiment thrown back to protect the flank."[32]

The countryside was heavily wooded, with many sudden dips and rises which created difficulty in viewing the field. The advance continued in good order over broken ground, when suddenly the brigade raised the rebel yell and broke into a run. Through the woods and across an open field they charged, excitement rising as the Yankees gave way under their onslaught. Through a boggy woods with thick underbrush and then into a second field, the Confederates charged on. They crossed six hundred yards of open field to route some Yankees barricaded behind a crude breastwork of rails near a log house (the Whitlock house). To the left of the house and behind it were two union batteries with four guns each. Kemper's men, seemingly unstoppable, stormed onward past the house and captured six of the eight guns.[33]

According to Private David E. Johnson of the Seventh Virginia, "the brigade met with a shower of shot, shell, and canister, and a storm of leaden bullets; it never faltered."[34]

The brigade moved on through the woods east of the clearing. The Seventeenth had to sidestep a swampy area and fell behind, but despite heavy fire on their flank, the First Brigade pushed onward, continuing their vigorous fire. The Federals on the other side of the clearing gave way to the sudden rush of Virginians, who were preceded by fleeing Yankee pickets.

The demoralized Federals fled the field in panic, leaving behind guns, knapsacks and other plunder. Kemper's brigade was now far in

32. Edgar Warfield *A Confederate Soldier's Memoirs* (Richmond, Virginia, 1936) p. 96.

33. Douglas Southall Freeman *R. E. Lee: A Biography* (New York, 1945) vol. II, pp. 186-190; Dowdey *Seven Days* pp. 298-299.

34. As quoted in Hitt, p. 45.

advance of any other Confederate unit. Brigadier General Micah Jenkins's and Cadmus Wilcox's brigades had not begun to advance until 5:40 PM, long after Kemper launched his attack. Brigadier General Lawrence O. Branch's brigade was still in a state of confusion and uncertainty. Brigadier General George E. Pickett's brigade finally moved forward in support of the valorous First Brigade, along with Brigadier General James J. Archer's brigade of Hill's Division. Pickett's troops passed through Kemper's lines and held the field. The First Brigade veterans did not take kindly to orders to fall back later that night.[35]

Kemper's losses in the battle of Frayser's farm were light, considering the amount of action they saw. One Yankee soldier wrote "On the 30th of June occurred that terrible action at Frayser's farm . . . the fighting qualities of those troops were so superior that they took batteries in hand-to-hand combat without the aid of a single gun."[36]

On July 2nd, the Yankees were in full retreat following the previous day's battle of Malvern Hill. Kemper's brigade was held in reserve and had no part in the fighting, but they did pursue the fleeing Yankees, reconnoitered the federal lines in preparation for a renewed attack and encountered union gunboats on the James River. The brigade returned to camp near Richmond on July 8th. The Seven Days Campaign was over.

The First Brigade spent the next month in camp and was strengthened by the arrival of conscripts and the exchange of prisoners of war. Company drill and picket duty occupied the men's time. The extreme heat and swampy conditions led to much sickness and disease.

Under Kemper's command, the First Brigade of Longstreet's Division had been conspicuous in action at Gaines's Mill and Frayser's Farm. Longstreet cited Kemper for "distinguished . . . gallantry and

---

35. Freeman *Lee* pp. 186-190; Dowdey *Seven Days* pp. 298-300; Hitt, p. 46.
36. Warfield, p. 96.

skill."[37]

On August 9, 1862, Kemper received orders to move his brigade at once, their destination—Gordonsville.[38] General Lee was about to move against another threatening foe, General John Pope, who was advancing from the north in the vicinity of Culpeper.

37.   O.R. Ser. 1, vol. XI, pt. 2, p. 759.
38.   O.R. Ser. 1, vol. 51, pp. 604-605.

Chapter 12

Manassas to Maryland and Back

General Lee reorganized the Army of Northern Virginia into two wings or corps and gave command of one corps to Stonewall Jackson. Jackson's corps consisted of two divisions, one under the command of Kemper's old friend A.P. Hill, the other under Longstreet. Longstreet's corps consisted of five divisions led by major generals Richard H. Anderson and David R. Jones; and brigadier generals Cadmus M. Wilcox, John Bell Hood, and James Lawson Kemper.[1]

Kemper was named acting division commander for an unspecified period of time upon Longstreet's promotion to corps command. Upon Kemper's temporary advancement, Colonel Corse became acting brigade leader; in his absence Lieutenant Colonel Morton Marye led the Seventeenth Virginia. In the absence of Colonel Funsten, who had been wounded the last day of May, the Eleventh Virginia was led by Major Adam Clement.[2]

Jackson defeated Pope's Union forces on August 9th at Cedar Mountain in Culpeper County, and Pope withdrew northward.

---

1.   n.a. *Lee Takes Command: From Seven Days to Second Bull Run* (Alexandria, Virginia, 1984) p. 92.
2.   Robert T. Bell *11th Virginia Infantry* (Lynchburg, Virginia, 1985) p. 29; Lee A. Wallace, Jr. *17th Virginia Infantry* (Lynchburg, Virginia, 1990) p. 37.

Kemper's troops broke camp on August 10th, when Longstreet's corps moved toward a railroad junction near Richmond. On the 13th they took the Virginia Central Railroad to Gordonsville, where they went into camp late that same evening.[3] Their orders were to join forces with Jackson's corps and defeat Pope's army before he could join forces with McClellan's army.

Kemper's division marched toward Orange Court House from Gordonsville under a broiling sun on August 14th, but were then ordered back through Gordonsville and into Louisa County, where they remained in camp for two days. On the 16th they marched north on the Orange and Fredericksburg Turnpike.[4] When they passed through Orange Court House, the men were greeted by General Kemper's aged mother, Maria, who waved and urged her son's troops on to victory. On the 20th they crossed the Rapidan River at Raccoon Ford. On the 21st the division halted and was held in reserve while a brisk cavalry and artillery engagement took place about one-half mile south of Kelly's Ford.[5]

While in camp, a federal spy dressed in a new Confederate uniform approached General Longstreet and presented to him a forged order, supposedly written by Stonewall Jackson, concerning troop movements. Longstreet knew all of Jackson's couriers, and it wasn't long before the identity of the spy was revealed. In just a few minutes he was swinging from a limb of a convenient tree.[6]

The division continued on past Stevensburg and through Brandy Station, up the Rappahannock, across the Hazel River to Jeffersonton, across the Rappahannock, and then to Salem and White Plains before halting at Thoroughfare Gap. They reconnoitered the area that evening, the 28th, in very close proximity to Pope's army. After dining on beef and green corn, the men slept,

---

3.   Loehr, p. 26; Riggs, p. 13.
4.   *Ibid.*, p. 26.
5.   *Ibid.*
6.   *Ibid.*, pp. 26-27.

64

only to be jarred awake by a stampede of escaped wagon horses which gave them the false impression that union cavalry was upon them.[7]

The Confederate soldiers were clad in rags, remnants of once-proud uniforms, and many were barefoot, their feet raw and bleeding. Nevertheless, the march resumed the next day. It was extremely hot that day, the roads dusty, and the soldiers thirsty. Longstreet's corps flanked the enemy out of Thoroughfare Gap and pushed on toward Manassas, where a battle had already erupted.[8]

Kemper's division halted three miles from Gainesville at noon and formed a line of battle. It was little more than a year since these men had fought on the fields of Manassas. Kemper had in addition to his own brigade, now under Corse, those of Colonel Eppa Hunton's Virginians and Jenkins's South Carolinians. Corse's brigade went into battle behind Jenkins and Hunton from a position east of the railroad. The Twenty-Fourth Virginia was detached to support Captain Arthur Rogers's Virginia battery. The rest of the brigade shifted to the west of the railroad and moved into a protected, wooded area to escape the constant shelling.

The Seventh Virginia was ordered forward as skirmishers as the battle line advanced. They were within sight of Jackson's corps, which was furiously battling Pope. Corse's brigade advanced but a short distance, then fell back and was relieved by Brigadier General Thomas F. Drayton's brigade. They took up a position near Groveton, where they spent the night.[9]

The next morning, August 30th, Longstreet's corps moved forward toward Manassas along a narrow country road bordered by a rail fence. Longstreet's order of battle was two brigades of Hood's division on either side of the turnpike; Brigadier General Nathan "Shanks" Evans's brigade in support; and Kemper's, Jones's, and

---

7. *Ibid.*, p. 27; Riggs, p. 13.
8. Hitt, p. 49; Riggs, p. 13.
9. *Ibid.*, p. 50.

Wilcox's divisions in column formation north of the turnpike. The men halted and rested until late afternoon.[10]

At 4:30 PM Longstreet ordered his corps forward. Corse's brigade was on the right of the division, behind Jenkins and Hunton. The division was to the left of Evans's South Carolinians. Their objective was the Chinn house on a commanding ridge about a half-mile away. The Confederates advanced under heavy musketry and artillery fire. By 5:30 PM the Ohio soldiers under union Colonel Nathan C. McLean were in desperate straits, suffering the combined attacks of Evans's brigade and Kemper's division.[11]

Kemper, personally leading his men, pushed past the Chinn house as the battle grew hotter by the minute. Kemper's old brigade charged a federal battery supported by the Eleventh Pennsylvania and overran it. "The men dashed forward in splendid style," wrote Captain Joseph Hambrick of Company B, Twenty-Fourth Virginia. They came upon a rail fence where Lieutenant Colonel Floweree of the Seventh called out to his men, "Up to the fence . . . and give them hell." Kemper continued the pursuit until late evening. The attack was brilliantly executed, but the division suffered heavy casualties, especially among the officers.[12]

Of the battle of Second Manassas, Private Alexander Hunter of the Seventeenth Virginia wrote, "[It] would make—were it not so terrible—a man love war and destruction for its noble excitement."

Kemper again attracted the attention of his superiors with his exemplary actions. Jeb Stuart wrote of Kemper's "good conduct, bravery, and coolness."[13] General Longstreet called Kemper the "most

---

10.   Edward J. Stackpole *From Cedar Mountain to Antietam: August-September 1862: Cedar Mountain—Second Manassas—Chantilly—Harper's Ferry—South Mountain—Antietam* (Harrisburg, Pennsylvania, 1959) p. 102.
11.   Hitt, p. 51; *Lee Takes Command,* p. 159.
12.   *Ibid.,* p. 51.
13.   O.R. Ser. 1, vol. XII, pt. 3, p. 738.

prominently distinguished officer at the battles of Manassas Plains."[14] Kemper had also won the praise and admiration of his men. His mother-in-law, Cremora Cave, wrote him, "You have made yourself dear to all your men. I do feel so glad where from every tongue, I learn something of your kindness and bravery."[15]

Kemper's division spent August 31st burying the dead, treating the wounded, and resting after the hard conflict. The march resumed on September 1st. Lee had seized the initiative, and he was determined to carry the war into northern territory. The weary troops marched for five days and reached White's Ford on the Potomac near Leesburg on September 6th. There Kemper's old brigade was attached to Jones's division, and Kemper returned to command it.

The army was in a poor state of affairs. Rations had been reduced to four ounces of bacon and two crackers daily to each man. They were still badly in need of shoes and clothing, and losses from battle had greatly reduced number of effectives in the ranks. Kemper's entire brigade numbered less than four hundred men. Losses among officers were so severe that the Seventh Virginia was now led by its captain, Philip S. Ashby, a Mexican War veteran.[16]

When the army crossed White's Ford, the bands struck up the familiar strains of "Maryland, My Maryland." Lee hoped to fill his ranks with new recruits from the border state, and the army was under strict orders to be on their best behavior. On September 10th, as Kemper's brigade marched through Frederick, their flag recently painted with the name of their great battle on the peninsula, several young ladies offered, "Three cheers for the battleflag of Seven Pines." The army was warmly welcomed in Maryland, but the number of new recruits was disappointingly low.[17]

Jones's division marched on to Hagerstown. On September 14th

14. O.R. Ser. 1, vol XI, p. 1, pp. 943-944.
15. Kemper papers, U.Va., letter from Mrs. Belfield Cave.
16. Riggs, pp. 14-15; Hitt, p. 53.
17. Hitt, p. 55.

they were ordered to support of Major General D.H. Hill at Turner's Gap. The march was very hot and dusty. Upon reaching their destination, Jones's division hurried up South Mountain to extend Hill's lines. Kemper's brigade and that of Brigadier General Richard Brooke Garnett were positioned on the ridge above and to the left of the pass. The Federals attacked, and the battle lasted for several hours. Although badly outnumbered, the Confederates held their position. Nightfall brought an end to the fighting, and the Confederates withdrew to the foot of the mountain.[18] Kemper was again recognized by Longstreet in his report, this time for his part in the battle of Boonsborough (now spelled Boonsboro).[19]

On the night of September 14th, Kemper's brigade began the march toward Sharpsburg, reaching their destination by noon of the next day. Along the way the men ate green corn and apples, the only food they had. At Sharpsburg the brigade was directed to the extreme right of the Confederate line. For two days the Southerners awaited the arrival of Jackson's corps from Harpers Ferry. Lee's army was outnumbered by McClellan's vastly superior force, but the ever cautious McClellan waited until the morning of September 17th to attack.[20]

The fighting raged out of sight of the Virginians, but they could tell all was going well for the Confederates as long as they could hear the rebel yell. The Twenty-Fourth was detached to the south around noon; the Seventh moved off to the other side of the Harpers Ferry Road, leaving only the First, Eleventh and Seventeenth Virginia regiments drawn up in line of battle on the extreme right flank of the southern army. At 3:30 PM Kemper's three small regiments secured a position behind a rail fence just beyond a small ridge at the edge of town. They rested while awaiting the coming attack, their muskets leaning against the rails, and took advantage of the brief

18.   *Ibid.*, p. 55.
19.   O.R. Ser. 1, vol. XII, pt. 3, p. 738.
20.   Riggs, p. 16.

pause to scribble a few lines home or get a drink of water.

Brigadier General Robert A. Toombs's Georgia brigade was in front of Kemper, on a bluff overlooking Antietam Creek. Toombs put up a gallant fight against union General Ambrose Burnside's overwhelming offense, but was driven back around 4:00 PM. Again and again the Georgians stayed the blue-clad columns trying to force their way across the small bridge, but eventually they could stand no more, and passed through Kemper's lines in retreat.[21]

Captain Ashby, still in command of the Seventh Virginia, told his men calmly, "Men, we are to hold this position at all hazards. If need be, we will die together here in this road."[22] Kemper's brigade was drastically reduced in strength; the Seventh, the largest, had just 117 men on line; the First, the smallest, had but 30. The brigade, less the Twenty-Fourth, numbered only 320 men.[23]

As the union troops approached the Virginians, Private Hunter described the scene:

> The first thing we saw appear was the gilt eagle that surmounted the pole, then the top of the flag, next the flutter of the stars and stripes itself, slowly mounting, up it rose, then their hats came in sight. Still rising the faces emerged, next a range of curious eyes appeared, then such a hurrah as only Yankee troops could give, broke the stillness, and they surged against us.[24]

With the lines only fifty yards apart, a sheet of flame and smoke erupted as both sides simultaneously fired a volley. The color guard of the Ninth New York fell as the Virginians raked the blue ranks

21. Warfield, pp. 116-117.
22. Hitt, p. 57.
23. *Ibid.*, p. 56; Warfield, p. 116.
24. Stephen W. Sears *Landscape Turned Red: The Battle of Antietam* (New York, 1983) p. 283.

with sweeping volleys. Bullets splattered against the rails as the Yankees fired into the Confederate lines. To the embattled Southerners, the fifteen seconds or so that it took them to reload seemed like an eternity. After ten minutes at most, the New Yorkers rushed the fence. In hand-to-hand combat, men were stabbed with bayonets, and muskets were swung as clubs. Despite their valorous effort, the vastly outnumbered Confederates were eventually forced to retreat. Private John Dooley of the First Virginia noted, "I was afraid of being struck in the back and I frequently turned half around in running, so as to avoid if possible so disgraceful a wound."[25]

Long lines of blue infantry pursued the fleeing Confederates, the air filled with bursting shells as union batteries opened. Just then there appeared on the road leading from Harpers Ferry a seemingly endless line of gray-clad troops marching under a proudly waving Confederate battleflag. In that instant, the whole scene changed.

Kemper's troops fell in with this new force (A.P. Hill, sent from Harpers Ferry by Jackson) and attacked the union line. Their combined effort drove Burnside's corps back, thus regaining all of the ground lost in the earlier fighting. They remained there until late afternoon of the following day. The anticipated a renewal of the federal attack never came.

The Confederates left the lines late on the 18th and marched to the river. The battle of Sharpsburg was over, and Kemper's brigade had again suffered heavily.[26] They waded the deep, cold waters of the Potomac at a ford a mile below Shepherdstown, then camped three miles from the river. From there, they marched to Winchester, where they spent considerable time recovering from the battle. There they were joined by many of the sick, wounded and shoeless men who had been left behind.

On October 6th, Kemper reviewed his troops at a camp near the

25.   *Ibid.*, p. 283.
26.   Warfield, pp. 118-120.

Hopewell meeting house, and praised them for their conduct during the Maryland Campaign.

Kemper, in his report on the campaign, brought special attention to the fact that his brigade had captured two stands of colors. Private Samuel S. Coleman of the Seventeenth Virginia seized a United States national flag from the color sergeant of the Eleventh Pennsylvania at Manassas on August 30th, and Lieutenant W.W. Athey of the Seventeenth snagged the regimental colors of the One Hundred Third New York at Sharpsburg on September 17th.[27] Kemper, in turn, was praised by General Longstreet in his report on the battle of Sharpsburg.[28]

Kemper, who possessed the qualities of a born leader, was loved and respected by his men. His "clear ringing [and] . . . clarion voice" was inspirational, and he was especially noted for his battlefield oratory. He cared for his men, believed strongly in the cause for which they were fighting, and was courageous and was cool under fire.

That fall the army was again reorganized, and Kemper's brigade was assigned to a new division of 4,194 men commanded by fellow Virginian George E. Pickett. The division was ordered to march to Culpeper Court House on October 28th and reached their destination on the 31st. They camped southeast of town for three weeks, enjoyed visits and gifts from local residents, and received many supplies from home. Gifts of clothing were especially appreciated as cooler weather approached.[29]

27.   O.R. Ser. 1, vol. 19, pt. 11, p. 677.
28.   O.R. Ser. 1, vol. XI, p. 1, pp. 943-944.
29.   Hitt, pp. 59-60.

Chapter 13

The Winter of 1862-63

General Pickett was of an old Virginia family and had served the Confederacy with distinction until he was wounded at the battle of Gaines's Mill. He resumed his brigade command upon his return to duty in September 1862, was promoted to major general on October 10th, and assigned to lead a new division, consisting of the First Brigade under Kemper (the First, Seventh, Eleventh, Seventeenth and Twenty-Fourth Virginia regiments); the Second Brigade under Garnett (the Eighth, Eighteenth, Nineteenth, Twenty-Eighth, and Fifty-Sixth Virginia regiments); and the Third Brigade under Brigadier General Lewis Armistead (the Ninth, Fourteenth, Thirty-Eighth, Fifty-Third, and Fifty-Seventh Virginia regiments).

While encamped at Culpeper Court House, the men drilled, received instruction, performed picket duty, and received new recruits and conscripts.[1] With the additional new troops, plus the return of convalescents and stragglers, the division numbered 9,000 men by the end of October.

Kemper's First Brigade was in good fighting order and had even improved its appearance. The men welcomed increased rations of beef and bread. Some clothing, shoes, tents and blankets were is-

---

1.   Walter Harrison *Pickett's Men: A Fragment of War History* (New York, 1870) pp. 64-65; Bell, p. 34.

sued, but despite the fact that local residents presented the men with supplementary clothing, many of the troops still lacked such necessities as boots, shoes and overcoats.[2]

On November 10th, the First Brigade was strengthened by the addition of the Third Virginia from Brigadier General Roger A. Pryor's brigade, which had been broken up. The new regiment was commanded by Colonel Joseph Mayo, Jr., and consisted of men primarily from the Portsmouth and Southside Virginia areas.[3] On the 19th of November, the division was ordered to Fredericksburg, a march of more than thirty miles.[4]

On October 26th, the Army of the Potomac under McClellan had begun an advance. In mid-November, President Lincoln removed McClellan, and General Burnside was placed in command. The new federal commander marched his army toward Fredericksburg, planning to cross the Rappahannock River there and engage Lee south of the historic old river town. Lee countered the move by directing his army toward Fredericksburg.

Kemper's men covered eighteen miles on the first day, a good bit of it ankle deep in mud. They waded the Rapidan River at Raccoon Ford, camped near Chancellorsville en route, and reached their new campsite, about two miles south of Fredericksburg, on November 25th. The ground was blanketed with about two inches of snow the day they arrived, but the site offered good wood and water. Their main activity for the next three weeks was cutting trees and building crude log huts for shelter.[5]

On December 2nd, Montgomery Corse, now a brigadier general, returned from furlough and accepted command of the new Fourth Brigade of Pickett's division, which had been created for him. At

2.   Bell, p. 34; Gunn, p. 37.
3.   Lee A. Wallace, Jr. *3rd Virginia Infantry* (Lynchburg, Virginia, 1986) p. 32.
4.   Morgan, p. 143.
5.   Wallace 17th Virginia Infantry p. 42; Riggs, p. 17.

his request, his old regiment, the Seventeenth Virginia, transferred from Kemper's command to his. The Fourth Brigade consisted of the Fifteenth, Seventeenth, Twenty-Ninth, Thirtieth, and Thirty-Second Virginia regiments.[6]

The camps of both armies stretched for some twelve or fifteen miles on either side of the Rappahannock. The Yankee camp was on Stafford Heights, overlooking Frederickburg and surrounding countryside. Their thousands of white tents were clearly visible from the Confederate-held hills on the south side of the river. The Yankees camped in open fields, but the Confederates, who seldom had tents, preferred the woods, where they could more easily improvise shelter.

The Confederate and union pickets along the river banks were always in sight of one another, but no firing occurred. They sometimes crossed over clandestinely and swapped tobacco for coffee. Newspapers were another scarce commodity, highly sought after by both sides.[7]

The lack of shoes continued to be problem for the Confederates. Rawhides from slaughtered cattle were distributed, from which the men were expected to make moccasin-like shoes, but this effort was a total failure. The crudely-made shoes had no soles, slipped badly in the snow and ice, and were quickly discarded. The men wrapped their feet in rags and straw.[8]

On December 11th, the Federals began to cross the Rappahannock River. Longstreet put Kemper's brigade on alert, and for the next two days the Virginians monitored this movement. On December 13th the brigade marched to the center of the Confederate line, just south of Fredericksburg, to support the Confederate troops preparing to engage the enemy. The Yankees, however, did not attack the center of the line but instead hit the left wing of Lee's

6. *Ibid.*, p. 42.
7. Morgan, pp. 143-144.
8. Gunn, p. 37.

defenses. Kemper moved his men off to the left at the double quick to support those being attacked. The brigade came under heavy artillery fire and soon broke into a run to get out of range.[9]

They crossed Hazel Run and moved onto Marye's Heights, a long hill overlooking the town of Fredericksburg. From this hill the troops were heard to exclaim, "Poor old Fredericksburg!" as they witnessed the terrible destruction heaped upon the old town. Lee had not planned to contest the river crossing by Burnside's forces seriuosly and sent only one brigade, that of William Barksdale, now a brigadier general. Several times the stubborn Mississippians drove back the Federals, who were trying to lay their pontoon bridge across the three hundred yards of river. The Yankees prevailed, however, after reducing most of the town to rubble with repeated artillery barrages.[10]

As the First Brigade moved into their reserve positions, Kemper delivered a "soul stirring address [that] had a good effect on the men." The day was so cold that frost formed in the beards of many. They shivered in the freezing fog without overcoats or boots, but were warmed by an inner fire when their commander promised, "If we can whip the enemy here today, I tell you from what I know, the Confederacy is surely established."[11]

Turning to the old First Virginia, a unit steeped in the finest tradition, Kemper declaimed, "Men of the First Virginia regiment— you who have on so many hard fought fields gained the name of the 'Bloody First'—today your country calls on you again to stand between her and the enemy, and I know you will do your duty."[12] To this the men of the First responded with "one of those yells that could be heard for miles."[13]

9.   Hitt, p. 62.
10.   Morgan, p. 146.
11.   *Ibid.*, p. 146.
12.   Loehr, p. 32.
13.   Lee A. Wallace, Jr. *1st Virginia Infantry* (Lynchburg, Virginia, 1985)

About 2:00 PM Longstreet ordered Pickett to send two brigades forward to support Brigadier General Robert Ransom's division, who were receiving the brunt of the attack. Kemper's Virginians and Jenkins's South Carolinians responded. It was almost dark when Kemper reported to Ransom. Two of Kemper's regiments, the First and Seventh, were sent to support troops fighting in the Sunken Road, and the Third was sent to relieve the Twenty-Fourth North Carolina, which had been on the line for forty-eight hours.[14]

The troops used their bayonets and tin cups to throw up crude breastworks. The enemy attacked in waves, with strong support, until 7:00 PM; the field in front of the Confederate line was alive with blue. Kemper's three regiments remained in position all night in anticipation of a renewed attack; his other regiments remained behind the front line in support. About 9:00 PM, the Twenty-Fourth relieved some of the battle-weary Confederates on the front line. Throughout the night the Virginians could hear the prayers, cries and curses of the wounded and dying federal troops lying on the field in front of them. The aurora borealis illuminated the battlefield with an eerie light. They could see clearly the piles of dead and wounded. Several of Kemper's men tried to take water to the wounded, but the Federals fired on anything that moved, and the officers were forced to order their men to stay in the trenches. The men got little rest that night as they lay among their dead compatriots.[15]

The only action during the night occurred about midnight, when a party of Yankee officers wandered too far while inspecting their picket lines and were captured by men of the First Virginia.[16]

The next day, a Sunday, Kemper's men were still in position be-

---

p. 37.

14.   Edward J. Stackpole *Drama on the Rappahannock: The Fredericksburg Campaign* (Harrisburg, Pennsylvania, 1957) p. 212; Wallace, *3rd Virginia Infantry* p. 33.

15.   Hitt, p. 62-63; Gunn, p. 38.

16.   Wallace, *1st Virginia Infantry* p. 37.

hind the stone wall in the Sunken Road, where they formed ranks, ready for battle at first light. As the mist cleared that morning, the Virginians directed a withering fire at a rail fence, which they mistook for advancing Yankee troops. Federal sharpshooters fired on them later that day, but they incurred few casualties, and at 10:00 PM they were relieved. The tired Virginians marched to the rear, where they rested for a day, and then set out on the 16th for Guiney's Station.[17]

General Lee, in his official report of the battle of Fredericksburg, wrote, "Brigadier General Kemper came upon the field late but in handsomest style, under a galling fire, moved his command into position with the greatest alacrity and steadiness, and during this time lost a few killed and quite a number wounded."

The brigade took up winter quarters in the woods just to the north of Guiney's Station, where they managed to make the best of a bad situation during the bitterly cold winter. Many of the men were still without shoes, and few of them had overcoats. To survive the cold nights, the men built fires to heat the ground, then extinguished them and slept on the still-warm earth. Rations, clothing and furloughs were exceptionally hard to obtain, yet the men remained in good spirits and seemed confident of eventual victory.[18]

Despite their own hardships and losses, the terrible destruction they had witnessed at Fredericksburg moved the Kemper's men to help the citizens of that devastated city. That winter the mayor of Fredericksburg received $2,291.50 raised by "subscription of the brigade to the sufferers of your city." The headquarters had yielded $170, the First $421, the Seventh $776, the Eleventh $401.50, the Twenty-Fourth $523, and the Third $505.[19]

In late January, the boredom was relieved by a large snowball

---

17. Gunn, p. 38.
18. Hitt, p. 63.
19. Letter from Kemper's brigade to Mayor of Fredericksburg, Fredericksburg National Military Park.

fight. The men of the Seventeenth Virginia spotted Toombs's Georgians sneaking into camp, their haversacks filled with snowballs. The Virginians rallied to meet the surprise attack, and soon there was an all-out battle. Officers led their men in attacks and counter-attacks, and prisoners of war were taken. When it was over, the men boasted of the late "campaign" and their part in the great "victory."[20]

On January 20, 1863, the brigade fell in and marched to Bank's Ford to counter a federal thrust across the river, but they never encountered the enemy. The weather was the most horrible of the entire winter, the frozen roads all but impassable for vehicles. They outmarched their supply wagons and spent the night without tents, food or fire. During the night, eight inches of snow fell. "The suffering was fearful," recalled one Virginian. Since the anticipated attack did not materialize, the cold, wet and exhausted men returned to camp at Guiney's Station.[21]

The loneliness and monotony of camp life was broken by numerous diversions. Music, card games, vaudeville skits and baseball, weather permitting, provided some diversion. Snowball battles became a favored activity. The casualty lists from these furious battles were often long, with bloody noses and bruises being the most common injuries.[22]

In mid-February Pickett's division was ordered to Richmond. Another campaign season was about to begin.

---

20. Hitt, p. 65.
21. *Ibid.*, p. 66.
22. Gunn, p. 40.

Chapter 14

The North Carolina Campaign

On February 16, 1863, Pickett's division, Kemper's brigade included, became the first unit in what would, for the next few months, become Longstreet's Department of Virginia and North Carolina. The Confederate War Department wanted protection for the capital and for the Petersburg and Wilmington & Weldon railroads, which carried supplies to Lee's army. Suffolk was already under federal occupation and the state of North Carolina was a likely target for federal aggression. With assurances that foraging would be easy, Longstreet's men began the long, miserable march toward Richmond, constantly battered with sleet and snow. One soldier noted that on this march, "the mud was deepest, the sky dullest, the weather gloomiest."[1]

They reached Richmond on the 19th and were met by enthusiastic citizens bearing food and drink aplenty. Some of the officers partook of exceedingly heavy volumes of alcohol, and several officers, including the dashing Colonel Floweree, were put under arrest by Kemper for being intoxicated.[2]

On Washington's birthday the men camped at Chester Station and awoke to find nearly a foot of fresh snow had fallen during the

1. Bell, p. 36; Riggs, p. 20; Hitt, p. 66.
2. Riggs, p. 20; Hitt, p. 66.

night. Never ones to waste an opportunity, Kemper's men insti-
gated another great snowball fight. Around March 1st, the camp
was relocated a mile southeast of Petersburg, where they remained
for about three weeks. It was a welcome respite for the battle-hard-
ened veterans, as this part of Virginia had, so far, escaped the rav-
ages of war. While in camp the men performed escort and picket
duties and enjoyed the hospitality of the local people. Captain
W.H. Morgan remarked that the splendid Virginia hams were, "the
finest I ever ate." Lieutenant Thomas V. Fry of Company A, Seventh Virginia, remembered it as, "a fine place for pies &c."[3]

On March 21st the brigade crowded into unheated boxcars of
the Petersburg Railroad bound for Goldsboro, North Carolina.
Since it was bitterly cold, the enterprising Virginians protected the
wooden floors with a layer of sand and built fires to keep warm.
The smoke was dense in the closed in cars and when they
de-trained at Goldsboro, on the Wilmington & Weldon Railroad
line, they were hailed as the "colored brigade."[4]

Rejuvenated by the fresh air, they marched to Kinston, arriving
in the deserted town on the 23rd. Many of the houses had been destroyed, a result of the union occupation. For two weeks the
brigade served as scouts and pickets, keeping a wary eye upon the
union troops while the Confederate commissariat gathered supplies. On the 29th, Kemper led the First and Seventh Virginia regiments on a reconnaissance mission to New Bern. One of his
officers later quipped that they had completed the venture "without
hurting anyone," after marching through mud and swamps for two
days.[5]

Although the North Carolina expedition was unpleasant for the
men, it proved to be useful for the Confederacy. While the Virginians protected the supply lines and kept the federal troops out of the

---

3.   Riggs, p. 20; Bell, p. 37.
4.   *Ibid.*, p. 21.
5.   *Ibid.*, p. 21.

state, other Confederate units collected valuable provisions—meat and grain for the men and forage for the animals. The brigade also received welcome issues of caps, jackets, pants, shirts, socks, shoes and some blankets and overcoats while in North Carolina.[6]

On the 4th the brigade returned to Kinston, where they received ample rations of rice, sweet potatoes, black-eyed peas and bacon. On the 5th, they boarded a train headed north, passed through Goldsboro and Weldon, and reached Franklin Station, Virginia, the following day. The weather had warmed up considerably, and some of the men rode on top of the boxcars to catch the breeze.[7] They stayed at Franklin for the next several days, glad to be back in Virginia again. Private Joshua Worrell of the Twenty-fourth Virginia described North Carolina as "the nearest to no place I ever saw. Low, flat and marshy and the most dismal swamps that I ever heard of."[8]

Longstreet then turned his attention from foraging in the Tar Heel State to the union garrison at Suffolk, Virginia. On the 11th, the brigade crossed the Blackwater River and marched for two days toward Suffolk. The men performed picket duty and awaited attacks that never materialized, but by holding the federal troops inside their lines, they again enabled other Confederate troops to gather supplies from the surrounding countryside. During the next several weeks there were daily skirmishes with federal pickets, which Colonel Patton of the Seventh Virginia described as "our only relief and diversion from the monotony of camp life."[9]

In late April, Lee sent word for Longstreet to move northward. At midnight on May 3rd, Longstreet's troops quietly slipped out of Suffolk and headed for Richmond on an all-night march through the swamps, often in waist-deep water. At mid-morning the brigade reached South Quay, where they rested the remainder of the day and

6.   Wallace *3rd Virginia* p. 34; Harrison, pp. 76-77.
7.   Hitt, p. 68.
8.   Gunn, p. 41.
9.   Riggs, p. 21.

learned of the great Southern victory at Chancellorsville. From there they marched to Chester Station, where the troops were saddened to learn of the death of Stonewall Jackson.[10]

The famed Stonewall had been wounded the night of May 2 by men of his own command. His left arm had been amputated, and the wounded general transported to the Chandler place at Guiney's Station to recuperate. His condition worsened, and at 3:15 PM on the evening of May 10, he called for A.P. Hill and spoke his last words, "Let us cross over the river and rest under the shade of the trees."

Kemper hurried to Richmond, where Jackson's body lay in state at the executive mansion and joined generals Longstreet, Ewell, Garnett and Corse, Provost Marshal Henry Winder and Commodore French Forrest as pall bearers for the fallen hero. They carried the body from the president's home to the capitol and the hall of the House of Representatives. The whole city turned out for the procession, which was led by a brass band and included the Nineteenth and Fifty-sixth Virginia regiments; General Pickett and his staff, all mounted; six pieces of artillery; a squadron of cavalry; the hearse, draped in black bunting and drawn by four white horses led by a servant; the pall bearers; one of Jackson's favorite horses led by a servant; a few soldiers of the old Stonewall Brigade; General Elzey and his staff; city of Richmond officials; President Davis in a carriage; the Confederate cabinet on foot; Governor Letcher and his aides; and a number of Virginia politicians. More than twenty thousand people filed by the flag draped casket. On the following Wednesday, Jackson began his final journey home by way of Gordonsville and Lynchburg to Lexington, where he was laid to rest.[11]

Kemper was often suggested that spring as a possible candidate for governor. Such talk raised outcries from newspapers and others all across the state, who argued that his place was in the field. Kem-

---

10.   *Ibid.*, p. 21.
11.   Burke Davis *They Called Him Stonewall: A Life of General T. J. Jackson, C.S.A.* (New York, 1988) p. 450.

per agreed.[12]

He rejoined his troops in camp at Taylorsville, where their time was devoted entirely to preparing for the next campaign. The men got badly needed rest and were refitted and supplied for the long march to come. The ranks were once more reinforced by the return of sick and wounded comrades and new recruits.[13]

A great religious revival swept through the camps at that time. The Reverend Doctor Theodore Pryor of the Presbyterian church devoted considerable time to holding religious meetings, at which twenty-five men of Kemper's brigade were converted.[14]

On June 3rd Lee began to concentrate his army for a second great invasion of the North. The great battles around Chancellorsville had been won without Longstreet and his legions, but soon they were to play an all-important role in the upcoming campaign of the Army of Northern Virginia.

12.   Jones, "Forgotten Virginian," p. 301.
13.   Hitt, p. 68; Riggs, p. 21.
14.   Rev. J. William Jones, D.D. *Christ in the Camp or Religion in Lee's Army* (Richmond, Virginia, 1888), p. 344; Hitt, p. 68.

Chapter 15

The March Northward

Pickett's division began its trek northward without two of its largest brigades; Jenkins's unit was left on the Blackwater River, and Corse's was detained at Hanover Junction to protect the railroads and bridges near Richmond. Despite repeated appeals to General Lee, Pickett was unsuccessful in having these brigades returned to his division. As the Pennsylvania campaign began, Pickett's division numbered about 4,700.[1]

As Lee's army moved toward Pennsylvania, Kemper's brigade was diverted to Tappahannock and King and Queen counties to scout a large body of union troops reported in the vicinity. The brigade crossed the Mattaponi River and marched toward Newtown in Essex County, but although the brigade remained in the area for several days, they returned to camp on June 7th without having seen the enemy.[2]

The next morning they marched toward Culpeper Court House and arrived there on the 10th. Lee's vast army, concentrated for the march northward, spread for miles around. Kemper's men camped near the town and were in excellent spirits as they prepared for the

---

1. Harrison, p. 79.
2. Wallace, *1st Virginia*, p. 41.

summer campaign.[3]

On June 14th, the brigade started forward in light marching order with three days' rations prepared. They marched toward Winchester by way of Gaines Cross Roads. On the 15th, they crossed the Shenandoah River at Quicken's Ferry, wading rapid waters nearly shoulder deep. The heat was frightful, the roads dusty. Sunstroke victims littered the wayside. On June 20th, they rested at Berryville, and the next day the men received a full supply of clothing.[4]

On the 24th, they left marched through Martinsburg and forded the Potomac at Williamsport, Maryland. Parched with thirst, weakened by exhaustion and covered with dust, hundreds again fell by the roadside during the long march. The next day they passed through Hagerstown, and on the 26th they crossed the Mason-Dixon line at Middletown, Pennsylvania.[5]

In Pennsylvania the weather changed, and pouring rains turned the roads into a slippery mire. On Sunday, the 27th, the brigade passed through Chambersburg, which appeared to be deserted. The few people they met had no great affection for the rebels, and more than a few maledictions were hurled at the men by sullen Yankee ruffians. The soldiers laughed off the defiance.

A group of young ladies gathered at the town square to deliver a verbal lashing to the audacious invaders, but the spirited Southern boys would have none of it. The Seventh Virginia regimental band drowned the protests of their northern antagonists with the strains of "Dixie." The men laughed, raised a rebel yell, and settled down in camp about two miles past Chambersburg on the Harrisburg Road.[6] Campaigning in Pennsylvania had been easy so far.

General Lee learned that the pursuing Yankee army, now under

3. *Ibid.*, p. 41; Hitt, p. 70.
4. *Ibid.*, p. 41.
5. *Ibid.*, p. 41.
6. *Ibid.*, p. 42; Riggs, p. 24.

the command of Major General George Meade, had crossed the Potomac, and he decided to concentrate his army, then scattered over most of five counties, for the possibility of a coming battle. Pickett's undermanned division was to become the army's rear guard, and the remainder of Longstreet's corps joined the massive concentration. On June 30th, Kemper's brigade was assigned the destruction of the Chambersburg and Harrisburg Railroad. Ties were piled and lighted to make huge bonfires, over which the rails were heated and then bent around trees, rendering them useless. The depot and other important buildings were destroyed. The following day the men rested.[7]

Kemper's men were relieved by General John D. Imboden's Confederate cavalry, and at 2:00 AM on July 2nd Pickett's division began a forced march toward Gettysburg, where a battle had begun the previous day. The route was rough, but the men once again marched rapidly under the broiling sun in the suffocating dust.[8] They were in superb shape, well disciplined and ready for a fight. Many had complained about their role as rear guard, afraid that they would miss action in what many believed would be the last great battle of the war.

The Virginians crossed South Mountain, and by 2:00 PM they had covered the twenty-three miles to the outskirts of Gettysburg. The exhausted men were welcomed by the sound of rumbling cannon and musketry as the battle continued to rage intensely. They camped near a stone bridge over Willoughby Run on the Cashtown Turnpike, three miles from Gettysburg. The men tensed in anticipation of combat, but they were not needed, and General Pickett was ordered to rest them for the coming day. Gradually the men relaxed, prepared their evening meal and fell off to sleep. As the day closed, the Virginians knew that tomorrow would bring them into

7.   Riggs, p. 24; Gunn, p. 42; Bell, p. 38.
8.   Bell, p. 38.

the maelstrom of combat.[9]

Before dawn on July 3, 1863, Pickett moved his division toward the field of battle. Kemper's First Brigade led the march, followed by Garnett's Second Brigade and then Armistead's Third Brigade. They crossed the open fields and moved to the southeast, through a valley, to join the Confederate lines at Seminary Ridge, which ran parallel to the federal line on Cemetery Ridge and concealed their formation from the enemy. The men loaded their weapons and stood for inspection in the rays of the rising sun. The weather was bright and clear; another hot day was in store.

The Virginians, posted in an orchard, nervously awaited their next orders, and before long Kemper's men began pelting one another with green apples. The mock battle halted when orders arrived sending them beyond a crest of the ridge to a fence, which they dismantled.[10]

Pickett was ordered to have his men lie down in battle formation in the open field. The battle plan called for an artillery barrage to knock out the federal long cannon, after which the infantry were to assault the enemy line about one mile away. By 7:00 AM the Confederates were in position, in full view of the enemy.

In Pickett's division, Kemper's brigade was on the right, with Garnett's brigade to their left and Armistead's brigade supporting them in the rear. Kemper's regiments were deployed from left to right: Third, Seventh, First, Eleventh and Twenty-Fourth.

Wilcox's North Carolina brigade was in line to Kemper's right, and Heth's division (under J.J. Pettigrew, as Heth had been wounded the day before) was off to Garnett's left. Isaac R. Trimble, leading Pender's division, was behind.

The Confederates, beginning to swelter beneath the hot sun, lay in position, facing the concentration of artillery on Cemetery Ridge

9.　　Gunn, p. 43; Bell, p. 38.
10.　　Bell, p. 38.

and the blue-coated infantry visible behind them. Charles M. Blackford of Lynchburg accurately predicted in his diary, "This will be a great day in history."[11]

---

11.   *Ibid.*, p. 39.

Chapter 16

"The Sun was Darkened"

As Pickett's Virginians awaited their next orders, General Lee rode before them. Kemper told his regimental leaders to pass word to the men that the commanding general had assigned the division the post of honor for that day. A little while afterwards every man in the ranks knew exactly what work had been cut out for them. They were to make no movement which might attract attention of their enemy, and at the sound of two signal guns they were to lie flat upon the ground.[1] There was an unusual absence of merriment among the men.[2]

Kemper's brigade numbered nearly 1,900 men. The old First Virginia, under Colonel Williams, counted about 240 men in its six companies. The Third Virginia, under Colonel Mayo, had 360 men in ten companies. The Seventh, under Colonel Patton, numbered 390 men in nine companies. The Eleventh was commanded by Captain James R. Hulter of Company H, because Major Otey had been arrested for drunkenness; it had about 430 men in ten companies. The brigade's largest regiment, the Twenty-fourth, had about 460 men in its ten companies.[3]

---

1.   Riggs, p. 24.
2.   Wallace, *3rd Virginia*, pp. 36-37.
3.   Kathleen R. Georg and John W. Busey *Nothing But Glory: Pickett's*

Kemper, who had gained a reputation in the army for his "solid qualities and sound judgement," looked very military in appearance that morning. Although somewhat thin-faced from the strain of forced marches and the nearly unbearable heat, he was resplendent in an impressive new uniform.[4]

At exactly 1:00 PM the signal guns fired, and the men fell flat on their faces. Colonel E. Porter Alexander, the commander of Longstreet's artillery, opened fire, "doing [his] best to match the very elements of heaven." The enemy's guns answered and their shells, intended for the Confederate artillery gunners, fell instead upon the infantry, inflicting heavy losses.[5] For the next two hours, the ground literally shook from the incessant fire of the 150 Confederate cannon and the return fire of even more Yankee guns.

Kemper's brigade was the most exposed of all. The men had had no time to entrench and were mainly lying in the open. One of them described what happened:

The atmosphere was rent and broken by the rush and crash of projectiles. . . . The sun, but a few minutes before so brilliant, was now darkened. Through this smoky darkness came the missiles of death. . . . The scene of carnage beggars description. . . . The men remained steadfast at their posts . . . [but] it must not be supposed that the men were not alarmed. . . . Many a poor fellow thought his time had come. . . . Great big stout-hearted men prayed, loudly too. . . . They were in earnest, for if men ever had need of the care and protection of our Heavenly Father, it was now.[6]

Division at Gettysburg (Hughstown, New Jersey, 1987), pp. 9-10.
4.   Clifford Dowdey _Death of a Nation: the Story of Lee and His Men at Gettysburg_ (New York, 1958), p. 268.
5.   Wallace _1st Virginia_, p. 42.
6.   Dowdey, p. 294.

John Dooley of the First Virginia wrote,

> Every now and then some companion would raise his head dis-
> figured and unrecognizable, streaming with blood, or would
> stretch his full length, his limbs quivering in the pangs of death.
> Orders were to lie as closely as possible to the ground, and I
> like a good soldier never got closer to the earth than on the pre-
> sent occasion.[7]

The losses in the division may have been as high as 500 from
this artillery cannonade. Kemper's brigade suffered about 15% casualties.[8] Sergeant-Major Johnston of the Seventh lay beneath an
apple tree during the barrage. As he raised his head to get a breath
of fresh air, Lieutenant Brown, lying close by, yelled, "You had
better get your head down, or you may get it knocked off." The
sergeant-major replied, "A man had about as well die that way as to
suffocate for want air." At that very moment a Yankee shell decapi-
tated two men and wounded three others, including the sergeant-
major and the lieutenant.[9]

Private Edward Howard Compton of Company B, Seventh Virginia wrote:

> [N]o tongue can tell or pen describe what took place in that
> time, the artillerymen working at an inch of their lives, loading
> and shooting as fast as they could. When one would be shot an-
> other would take his place. The jar of cannons and bursting of
> shells shook the earth, it seemed the ground was thrown up.
> Pieces of shells was filling the air, men was falling in every di-
> rection. Then was the trying time on the Infantry who were

7.   Wallace *1st Virginia*, p. 42.
8.   George R. Stewart *Pickett's Charge: A Microhistory of the Final Attack at Gettysburg, July 3, 1863* (Dayton, Ohio, 1983), p. 139.
9.   *Ibid.*, p. 140.

lying flat on the ground with a broiling sun beaming down [on] them, seemingly the hottest that ever shone from the heavens. Our loss was immense, the litter bearers were unable to move the disabled, say nothing of the dead.[10]

Kemper described General Longstreet during the cannonade as the "grandest moral spectacle of the war." He wrote:

I expected to see him fall every instant. Still he moved on, slowly & majestically, with an inspiring confidence, composure, self-possessing and repressed power, in every movement and look that fascinated me. As he neared me, I walked up to him, intending to remind him of his peril of which he seemed really unconscious, and said, "General, this is a terrible place." Said he, "What! Is your command suffering?" "Yes," I answered, "a man is cut to pieces here every second while we are talking; sometimes a dozen are killed by one shot."

In describing the shelling, Kemper reported that the shells "pelted them and ploughed through them, and sometimes fragments of a dozen mangled men were thrown in and about the trench left by a single missile."[11]

At 1:40 PM, Colonel Alexander advised General Pickett to advance. Once Longstreet consented to the charge, Pickett rode among his men and exclaimed: "Up men, and to your posts! Don't forget that you are from old Virginia!" With everything ready, Pickett dispatched a volunteer aide, Captain Robert A. Bright, to Kemper with instructions.

---

10.   E. H. Compton *Reminiscences of Edward Howard Compton: A Survivor of Second Battle of Manassas and the Battle of Gettysburg* (Front Royal, Virginia, n.d.), p. 11.
11.   Letter from Kemper to Edward Porter Alexander, September 20, 1869, as quoted in Georg, p. 41.

As Kemper rose to meet the captain, he removed a handkerchief from under his hat; it had protected his eyes from dirt and dust during the cannonade. Bright reined up and delivered his orders. "[You are to dress on Garnett and take the red barn for . . . [your] objective point.[12] General Pickett orders you to advance your brigade, immediately."[13]

Private Compton described the scene as the brigade moved out:

"[W]e were ordered forward which was welcomed as a change if not a relief from the ordeal through which we had passed. At word forward we started, passed over Wilcox's men who pittied us saying 'Boys, that's a hot place. We were there yesterday.' Lee, Longstreet, Pickett were all there sitting on their horses when we started."[14]

There was no cheering, no rebel yell as the attack began, only a resolute determination to take the enemy position. The ordeal ahead would soon make them forget the fearsome artillery duel they had just endured.

12.　Gunn, p. 45.
13.　Georg, p. 64.
14.　Compton, p. 13.

Chapter 17

Nothing But Glory

The skirmishers were deployed 200 yards in advance of the main assault line. Kemper's men moved eastward "deliberately and in good order." They crossed the double fence at Spangler's Lane and quickly reformed the line. Across the plain below they continued in parade ground formation. The brigade never looked better. As they climbed out of a ravine and neared the Emmittsburg Road, they came under devastating fire from Colonel Benjamin Rittenhouse's battery on Little Round Top, then Colonel Freeman McGilvery's battery opened up on the exposed flank of the Twenty-fourth Virginia, an inviting target which the union artilleryists hit with supreme accuracy. This withering artillery fire was just the beginning.[1]

As they crossed the Emmittsburg Road, Kemper's and Garnett's brigades parted. Kemper was to pass to the south of the Nicholas Codori farmhouse and barn, Garnett to the north. Kemper rode among his troops, encouraging his men and talking to his officers. He was reported to have had about him a "curious calm . . . and sense of leisure."[2]

Kemper rode over to Armistead to deliver some message. R.A.

---

1. Gunn, p. 45.
2. Jones, "Forgotten Virginian," p. 304.

Brock, a regimental officer, later reported that "the impetuous Kemper . . . cantered down . . . the front of Armistead's brigade on his sorrel. . . . [T]he men greeted him with a rousing cheer, which I know made his gallant heart leap for joy."[3]

The artillery fire picked up. Kemper's brigade received head-on artillery fire from Captain J.M. Rorty's guns and full enfilade from Rittenhouse's, as well as raking fire from the batteries of Captain Daniels and Colonel McGilvery.[4]

Pickett's grand division pressed onward, maintaining their parade ground appearance. With dressed lines, mounted officers riding back and forth among the men, and the flag waving smartly, they made an impressive sight.[5] Kemper's brigade passed the south side of the Codori house as ordered, then met the union infantry in force. The Vermont brigade of General George Stannard, clustered in a grove of trees southeast of the farmhouse and perpendicular to the union line, took full advantage of Kemper's exposed flank.[6]

Pickett, upon seeing the punishment taken by the brigade, sent repeated messages to Wilcox and Brigadier General James Henry Lang to come up and protect the exposed men.[7] Despite the heavy fire, the Virginians pressed on. They soon received frontal fire from General William Harrow's and General N.J. Hall's union brigades, and more raking fire from Colonel Theodore Gates's regiment. The union gunners then bombarded the Virginians with canister. Kemper, apparently acting against orders, led his men on horseback through the fray.[8]

The original orders that morning decreed that no officer was to

---

3.   *Ibid.*, p. 305.
4.   Stewart, p. 186.
5.   Dowdey, *Death of a Nation*, p. 198.
6.   Gunn, p. 46.
7.   Glenn Tucker *High Tide at Gettysburg: The Campaign in Pennsylvania* (Dayton, Ohio, 1983), p. 361.
8.   Georg, p. 105.

ride into the charge, as a mounted man would make too good a target.[9] Only General Garnett was given specific permission to ride into battle, because of illness that prohibited him from walking. Nevertheless, Kemper rode, as did colonels Terry and Williams. Kemper's aide-de-camp, First Lieutenant George E. Geiger; his assistant adjutant and inspector general, Captain Thomas Gordon Pollock; and his orderly, private George Walker of Company C, Eleventh Virginia, rode with him.[10] Already some of the mounted men were down.[11]

The men marched in a half stoop, their heads bowed forward as if weathering a storm. Here and there they moved a little, only to be blasted by rifle fire.[12] Kemper rode among them, keeping up their morale. He took time to ride up to the Codori house, where he inquired about Major Edmund Berkley of the Eighth Virginia, who had been terribly wounded.[13]

Kemper's brigade had received the bad end all day. Now they faced a devastating outburst of rifle fire from the front and oblique. Smoke covered the field and added to the confusion. Men were falling, several officers were down, the left guide was down, and a gap began to open between Kemper's and Garnett's brigades.[14] Still, the men didn't break.

Kemper received orders from George Hammer, an orderly to Colonel Hunton, to dress on Garnett's right, which forced him to shift position slightly.[15] The gap was filled, and Kemper's men mingled with Garnett's, but still they pressed onward. Armistead's brigade, the largest, overlapped Kemper and Garnett. Armistead

9.   Stewart, pp. 202-204.
10.   Georg, p. 208.
11.   Stewart, p. 198.
12.   *Ibid.*, pp. 198-202.
13.   Georg, p. 117.
14.   Stewart, pp. 200-205.
15.   Georg, p. 79.

was determined to follow where led, and his men pressed on, following the lead brigades which were "moving like waves on the sea."[16]

Garnett's brigade opened fire, and almost simultaneously Kemper's did likewise. Kemper spun his horse around and called to Armistead, "[H]urry up! I am going to charge those heights and carry them, and I want you to support me." Armistead answered, "I'll do it, look at my line, it never looked better on dress parade."[17]

Private Compton described the action:

[T]he shot and shells were sweeping the face of the earth. We took our place in the reg't—just before we reached the brick house. It was here that the Infantry opened fire on us and the artillery in our front into our lines. Grape and canister mow[ed] down our men like grass before scythe. . . . Still onward this line of Virginians pressed, who up to that day had never known defeat.[18]

Kemper stood in the stirrups and pointing with his sword, called out to his men, "There are the guns, boys, go for them!"[19] The men gave the rebel yell and surged forward, into even more devastating fire. Kemper turned to Armistead, calling out, "General, hurry up, my men can stand no more."[20] The brigade drifted even further to the left.

Kemper later said of his men that day:

"I never saw the behavior of men in battle equal to that shown by my command in this advance. The danger to be met was

16.   *Ibid.*, p. 89.
17.   Dowdey, *Death of a Nation*, p. 318; Georg, p. 90.
18.   Compton, p. 17.
19.   Stewart, p. 205.
20.   Tucker, p. 362.

plainly visible. It was as well calculated to terrify as any mortal eye ever saw. . . . At the most critical moment, our line was a dress-parade line and the marching was beautifully exact."[21]

Within one hundred yards of the union line, a bullet hit Kemper in the groin and drove upward into his body. He tumbled backward from his sorrel into the arms of his orderly, who gently lowered the wounded general to the ground.[22]

The wound was excruciatingly painful,[23] but Kemper remained in charge. His men fired one well-directed volley, then charged the enemy works, carried forward by the famous rebel yell. Soon after Kemper was hit, General Garnett fell mortally wounded at the stone wall. With both Garnett and Kemper down, Armistead took charge of the advancing troops. Stepping in front of the line with his hat on the point of his sword, he led the Virginians over the wall where he, too, fell, just inside the enemy lines.[24]

Pickett's Charge was over.

---

21.   Letter from Kemper to Edward Porter Alexander, September 20, 1869, quoted in Georg, p. 91.
22.   *Ibid.*, p. 98.
23.   Letter from Kemper to John B. Botchelder, February 4, 1886, as quoted in *Ibid.*, p. 98.
24.   *Ibid.*, p. 123.

Chapter 18

Aftermath of the Battle

Kemper's staff huddled around that bleeding, suffering officer.[1] Some time after the War, Kemper described his wounding to his compatriot, David Johnson:

> I think General Garnett and myself were the only officers of Pickett's division who went into that battle mounted and remained mounted until shot down. My recollection is that I fell just about the time our men began to give back. I was close enough to the enemy to distinguish features and expressions of faces, and thought I observed and could identify the individual who shot me. Quickly afterwards a federal officer with several of his men took possession of me, and placing me on a blanket started to carry me, as he said, to a federal surgeon, when some of our men, firing over my body, re-captured me and carried me to our rear.
>
> As to how the three brigades of our division advanced in line of battle when the artillery ceased firing; as to how the gaps were closed up as men fell and the general alignment was well pre-

---

1.   Jones, "Forgotten Virginian," p. 307.

served; as to the cul-de-sac of death our unsupported or very badly supported division was hurled into; as to the last availing and tragical grapple with the overwhelming numbers of the enemy; all these are matters about which you doubtless know as much as I do.[2]

The ill-fated charge nearly destroyed the division. Besides the three brigadiers, every colonel and lieutenant colonel was shot down.[3] Colonel Mayo took command of the remnants of Kemper's brigade.[4] They retreated to the Confederate lines along Pitzer's Run, where the walking wounded bathed their wounds, making its clear water run red. About 300-400 men were gathered there when General Pickett rode up. Corporal Charles Belcher of the Twenty-fourth Virginia called out, "General, let us go at them again." The wounded General Kemper was carried into this throng.[5]

Pickett burst into tears as Lee rode up. The two shook hands as Pickett said, "General Lee, I have no division now. Armistead is down, Garnett is down, and Kemper is mortally wounded."[6] Lee replied, "General Pickett, your men have done all that men could do; the fault is entirely my own."[7]

Lee then turned to Captain Bright, who was helping the litter bearers with Kemper. "What officer is that you are bearing off?" Bright replied, "General Kemper, sir." Lee walked up closer. "I must speak to him." Kemper opened his eyes and stared clear-eyed at Lee.

---

2.   David E. Johnson *Four Years a Soldier* (Charleston, West Virginia, 1887), pp. 258-259.
3.   G. Moxley Sorrell *Recollections of a Confederate Staff Officer* (New York, 1905), p. 172.
4.   Georg, p. 151.
5.   *Ibid.*, pp. 185-186.
6.   Shelby Foote *The Civil War: A Narrative (Fredericksburg to Meridian)* (New York, 1963), p. 568.
7.   Georg, p. 186.

"General Kemper, I hope you are not very seriously wounded."

"I am struck in the groin and the ball has ranged upward. They tell me it is mortal."

"I hope it will not prove so bad as that. Is there anything I can do for you, General Kemper?"

"Yes, General Lee, do full justice to this division for its work today."

Lee replied in a low voice, "I will," then walked away with his head bowed.[8]

Kemper was carried away from the battlefield by ambulance. While traveling down Pitzer's Lane, on the way to a field hospital, the ambulance was toppled by a union shell, and the wounded general was thrown to the ground. The driver and private Erasmus Williams of the Fourteenth Virginia carried him on a blanket on to a makeshift hospital on Willoughby Run, along the Fairfield Road.[9] The farm owner, Francis Bream, had Kemper brought into his spacious home. The wounded men in the farmer's barn could hear the general's cries and groans as he suffered "almost beyond endurance."[10] The doctors' prognosis was not good; the wound was almost certainly mortal and a coffin was ordered built for him. Throughout the night Kemper suffered tremendously, and his wounds bled profusely.[11] (Twenty-two years later his bloodstains were still distinctly visible on the floor of the house.)[12]

Kemper was still alive on July 5th when the Confederate army headed south. A week later he fell into federal hands, "still suffer-

8.   Dowdey *Death of a Nation*, p. 331; Georg, p. 186; Garry W. Gallagher *Fighting for the Confederacy: The Personal Recollections of General Edward Porter Alexander* (Chapel Hill, North Carolina, 1989), p. 266.

9.   Georg, p. 188.

10.   *Ibid.*, p. 188; Johnson *Confederate Boy*, p. 218.

11.   Jones "Forgotten Virginian," p. 310.

12.   Johnson *Confederate Boy*, p. 218.

ing severely."[13] General Meade wrote of the capture of Kemper "mortally wounded on the road to Fairfield."[14]

It was generally believed that Kemper had died. General Lee sent his condolences to Kemper's widow, and newspapers all over the South carried stories of his death, but the steadfast Belle Kemper refused to believe those stories.[15] The family hoped the general would be on one of the wagons of the 17-mile-long train of wounded from the battle of Gettysburg that took an entire day to pass through Orange Court House, but he was not.[16]

When it was certain that Kemper hadn't been brought South, his brother John and brother-in-law William F. Botts started for Pennsylvania to find him. In Winchester they met some men from Madison, who told them that he was certainly dead.[17]

Three weeks after the battle, however, Kemper had been taken to a hospital set up in the Lutheran seminary in Gettysburg.[18] There he was confined in a room with General Isaac Trimble, who had lost a leg in the charge; Major Henry Kydd Douglas, formerly of Stonewall Jackson's staff; and Colonel Robert M. Powell of the Fifth Texas Infantry. Two militiamen were posted at the door to guard the Confederate officers. Douglas and Powell were able to move about, but Kemper's and Trimble's wounds kept them immobile.[19]

The rules regulating the prisoners were strict, but one day some ladies were permitted to visit the officers. They declared to Kemper

13. Jones, "Forgotten Virginian," p. 310.
14. O.R. Ser. 1, vol. XXVII, pt. 1, p. 80.
15. Jones, "Forgotten Virginian," p. 311.
16. Allen Gray Dunnington *Forgotten as a Dream: Remembrances of a Virginia Lady* (Orange, Virginia, 1990), p. 18.
17. Letter from Maria R. Botts as quoted in Jones, "Forgotten Virginian," p. 311.
18. Georg, p. 189.
19. Col. Robert M. Powell *Recollections of a Texas Colonel at Gettysburg* (Gettysburg, Pennsylvania, 1990), p. 31.

their hostility toward all Confederates and their Cause. Kemper winked at Powell, then easily won over the unionist ladies with his charm and sparkling conversation. Women, not war, was his theme, and soon the ladies were in a fantasy land where the sole role of women was to administer to the afflicted. The ladies forgot their mission and moved closer to the general, one fanning him to cool his fevered brow, another bathing his parched and burning hands as Kemper quoted Sir Walter Scott, "Oh, woman, in our hours of ease." With this excited effort, he lapsed into a state of painful weariness. Handkerchiefs dried tears of sympathy as the ladies bade him a reluctant farewell with a reminder to "love your enemies."[20]

Another time, when visitors had been forbidden to visit with the prisoners in their rooms, two ladies who breeched the rules to visit with Kemper were stopped by the guards, who attempted to detain them for violating orders. Kemper, seeing the predicament his lady friends were in, called out to a nearby Confederate officer and a private, "Kill them! Kill them!" Armed with a penknife, they charged the militiamen, who fled in the face of the minor onslaught. The ladies escaped and took the contraband pen knife with them. The guards returned with a captain and a squad of militia to disarm the prisoners. They searched the quarters but found no weapon, and the captain ordered the hapless guards to be incarcerated.[21] Thus the wounded Kemper won two victories in the North!

On August 18th, Kemper left the seminary, and on August 22nd he was admitted as a patient to the United States Army General Hospital at Newtown University in Baltimore. Two days later he was turned over to the provost marshal at Fort McHenry as a prisoner of war. His family learned from Richard Norris, an exile from Baltimore, that Kemper wasn't dead.[22]

---

20.   *Ibid.,* p. 34.
21.   *Ibid.,* p. 34.
22.   Jones, "Forgotten Virginian," pp. 310-312.

Belle Kemper urged the Confederate authorities to try to have her husband exchanged, and on September 12th Robert Ould, the Confederate commissioner of prisoner exchanges, arranged for Kemper to be exchanged for Brigadier General Charles K. Graham, U.S.A., who was also a Gettysburg casualty.[23]

On September 17th, Kemper boarded a boat in Baltimore for Fortress Monroe, and the exchange took place on September 22nd.[24] After a long, painful and trying ordeal, Kemper returned home to his family in Madison, where he would spend the next several months recuperating from his wounds.

23. *Ibid.*, p. 313; Georg, p. 189.
24. *Ibid.*, p. 313.

Chapter 19

Return to Duty

Kemper was greeted as a hero by his family and friends in Madison. His homecoming was bittersweet, however, since his eldest daughter, Frances, had died of natural causes while he lay wounded in the makeshift hospital at Gettysburg.[1] Kemper was a physical wreck, unable to walk without the aid of crutches and in almost constant pain. He described his injury in a letter to his brother-in-law, John Holmes Bocock:

> I was struck by a minie-ball upon the inside of the left thigh near the femoral artery—the ball glancing up the thighbone, passing through the cavity of the body and lodging near the base of the spine—where it still remains. At first the lower half of my body was paralyzed.[2]

The grievous wound rendered him prostrate for more than a month after the battle, but upon his return home it began to heal

---

1. Robert Rivers Jones "Conservative Virginian: The Postwar Career of James Lawson Kemper" (University of Virginia, Ph.D. Dissertation, 1964) p. 9; Kemper papers V.H.S.; Kemper and Wright *Genealogy*.
2. Kemper papers V.H.S., Kemper to John Holmes Bocock October 6, 1863.

rapidly. In October Kemper wrote that he was "getting well but still suffering more or less," and he had "entirely recovered except that my left leg is still nearly helpless."[3] Although shaken badly by the injury, his quick recovery filled him with hope, and by the first of the year he informed his sister Sarah that he needed "nothing but the right sort of occupation to be almost as well as ever."[4]

Unfortunately, the initially rapid rate of improvement soon dropped off, and he never completely regained full use of his left leg. Travel by horseback caused him considerable pain. He was unable to walk without a cane and had a pronounced limp the rest of his life. He remarked that he was "seriously and permanently disabled by wounds received in battle."[5]

While home on leave recuperating, Kemper actively recruited for the Confederate service. Once, in front of the county court house, he spoke with fiery zeal about battles he had been in. "And the Confederate flag was held aloft until the bearer was shot down, but before the flag touched the ground, another soldier grasped it and held it high until he, too, fell in battle!" Instead of inspiring a patriotic fervor as intended, he got exactly the opposite response from one old mountaineer who called out from the back of the crowd, "Tain't no recommend to me!"[6]

That winter Kemper felt well enough to once again offer his services to the Confederacy. On January 22, 1864, he wrote General Lee, urging that he "call out the full resources of the country."[7]

He returned to his brigade in the early spring. It must have been a difficult and trying time for him, as he desperately wanted to do his

3.   Kemper papers V.H.S., Kemper to John Holmes Bocock, October 6, 1863.
4.   *Ibid.*, Kemper to Sarah Bocock, January 22, 1864.
5.   Amnesty papers National Archives, Kemper to President Andrew Johnson, July 1, 1865.
6.   Dunnington, p. 18.
7.   O.R. Ser. 1, vol. 33, p. 1127.

part for the war effort, but was physically unable to command a fighting unit in the field.[8] General Lee was undoubtedly troubled over Kemper's situation. He wrote to his son, General George Washington Custis Lee, in early April, "I believe [it] will turn out for the best. I have a high opinion of General Kemper."[9]

On April 25, 1864, Pickett's division was ordered to capture Washington and New Bern, North Carolina. Kemper wanted to command his brigade, but he wasn't up to the rigors of active duty.[10] Colonel Terry commanded the brigade in Kemper's absence.

On April 30th, Special Order 101 from the Confederate War Department assigned "Brigadier General James Lawson Kemper . . . to the command of the reserve forces of the State of Virginia, enrolled and mustered into service."[11]

When his brigade returned from North Carolina, Kemper delivered his farewell address to the men of the First, Third, Seventh, Eleventh, Seventeenth and Twenty-fourth Virginia regiments. "It were enough of honor to have shared the fortunes of any one of these regiments. . . . [T]he God of Battles steel your nerves and shelter your forms amid the perils of the field."[12]

Colonel Terry was promoted to brigadier general and given permanent command of the brigade. Kemper had nothing but praise for him as "an able disciplinarian, talented, brave, and extremely popular with the whole command. . . . He has often been distinguished for his coolness and efficiency in battle."[13]

Earlier that year, on February 17, 1864, the Confederate States

---

8.   Jones "Forgotten Virginian," p. 314.
9.   Clifford Dowdey ed. *The Wartime Papers of R. E. Lee* (Boston, Massachusetts, 1961), p. 696.
10.   Edward Younger ed. *Inside the Confederate Government: the Diary of Robert Gaslick Hill Kean, Head of the Bureau of War* (New York, 1957), p. 145.
11.   O.R. Ser. 1, vol. 51, p. 881.
12.   Riggs, p. 32.
13.   Wallace *3rd Virginia*, p. 47.

Congress passed an act extending the conscription age to include all white men between the ages of 17 and 50. Those between 18 and 45 were enlisted for the duration of the war; those under 18 and over 45 were to constitute the reserves.[14]

On May 7th, Kemper was detached from his brigade by Special Order Number 107 and given command of all the reserve forces of the state, with headquarters in Lynchburg, and ordered to complete their organization and place them at once into service.[15] Special Order 113 ordered all quartermaster, commissary, ordnance, and medical department officers to furnish all troops and facilities and all officers of Virginia militia, invalid corps, and unassigned troops to report to Kemper.[16]

Kemper set about immediately to see that "every man able to walk or render any service whatsoever" be enlisted for service.[17] All summer Kemper worked tirelessly to bring those claiming exemption from service into duty. On July 22nd, acting upon the recommendation of Kemper, the War Department announced that all detailed men, including those 18 to 45, would be organized into companies to be armed, disciplined, and regularly drilled.[18] Detailed men were those skilled at various trades who had been sent from the army to work in government foundries, workshops, and depots.[19]

During that summer all the remaining militia companies were placed under Kemper's control; he placed them under the immediate command of Brigadier General Patrick T. Moore, commander of the Rendezvous of Reserves in Richmond.[20] Also placed under Kemper's command was a regiment of foreigners "who have rendered

---

14.   Wallace *Guide . . .*, p. 218.
15.   *Ibid.*
16.   O.R. Ser. 1, vol. 35, pt. 2, p. 1012.
17.   Jones "Forgotten Virginian," p. 316.
18.   Wallace *Guide . . .*, p. 218.
19.   *Ibid.*, p. 179.
20.   *Ibid.*, p. 237.

themselves liable to do military duty by voting in the Confederacy, but are at the same time permitted to remain in Richmond as shoemakers, blacksmiths, etc."[21]

Kemper also commanded the corps of cadets from Virginia Military Institute. The cadets had served honorably in May of 1864 at the battle of New Market. That summer they were in Richmond, where they would serve as part of the defenses of Richmond until called back to Lexington to repulse the invasion of union General David "Black Dave" Hunter.[22]

Kemper took to the field twice that summer himself. In May he personally led all the forces he could muster—including old men, boys, and semi-crippled veterans—to repulse General Philip Sheridan's attack near Yellow Tavern, just a few miles north of Richmond. Kemper and his men stopped Sheridan with the aid of some old smoothbore artillery pieces.[23] In late June, when the Southside Railroad was threatened by advances made by Yankee cavalry, General Lee telegraphed to General Braxton Bragg, "Let Genl. Kemper collect what reserves he can at the threatened points at once."[24] The reserves were able to repulse the threatening Yankees.

General Kemper believed in vigorous enforcement of the Conscription Act,[25] but realized it was nearly impossible to bring the armies up to strength because of so many men claiming exemption. On September 10th, General Lee wrote to General Bragg, "I was informed by General Kemper that in this state alone there were no less than forty thousand exempts, details and applications for detail yet

---

21. *Ibid.*, p. 260.
22. *Ibid.*, p. 230.
23. Clifford Dowdey Lee's *Last Campaign: The Story of Lee and His Men Against Grant-1864* (New York, 1960), p. 221.
24. Dowdey, *Wartime Papers . . .*, p. 803.
25. Douglas Southall Freeman *R. E. Lee: A Biography* (New York, 1945), vol. III, p. 498.

undecided."[26] Kemper recommended the president have an inspection made of the conscription service, "I think the department should be filled by the best capacity and the greatest vigor and industry that can be obtained, and should be confined to the single duty of putting men in the army."[27]

In a report to Adjutant General Samuel Cooper on September 16th, Kemper reported that the reserve forces of Virginia were well organized, armed, equipped and trained. The force was comprised of five brigades embracing nineteen regiments and battalions as well as detached companies. The brigades averaged 2,600 men each, for a total of 13,072 officers and men.[28]

On September 19, 1864, Kemper was promoted to major general.[29] He continued his aggressive program to press men into service, and the remaining companies of second class militia were placed in his command. He at once put them to guarding union prisoners at Castle Thunder, the Richmond city jail, and providing security for railroad bridges and the Treasury Department.[30] In October, the cadets from V.M.I. returned to Richmond to help defend the city.[31]

Kemper was now providing what was perhaps his most valuable service to the Confederacy. Through his efforts in these last months of the war, Lee's army was strengthened by as many as 40,000 men. Kemper was also active in helping his friends during this time. He appealed on behalf of an elderly Ebenezer Goss:

---

26. Dowdey, *Wartime Papers . . .*, pp. 851-852; Bruce Catton *Never Call Retreat* (Garden City, New Jersey, 1965), p. 403.
27. *Ibid.*, pp. 851-852.
28. O.R. Ser. 4, vol. III, pp. 654-655; "William 'Extra-Billy' Smith, Governor of Virginia 1864-65: A Pillar of the Confederacy" by Alvin A. Fahner *Virginia Magazine of History and Biography* vol. 74, no. 1, January 1966, p. 71; Wallace *Guide . . .*, p. 218.
29. Jones, "Forgotten Virginian," p. 314.
30. Wallace, *Guide . . .*, p. 262.
31. *Ibid.*, p. 231.

Hd-qers R F Va
22nd Oct. 1864

Col. W. H. Taylor
Cv. a. y. Hd-qer A.N.V.
Colonel:

I respectfully ask your special attention to the case of Ebenezer Goss, who, under strict enforcement of orders has been assigned as a recruit to the 19th Va Infantry, H _____ Brigade, Pickett's Division. He is a very valuable man, an excellent gentlemen, but growing old and corpulent and not suited for Infantry service. I earnestly ask that he be trans. to 4th Va Cavalry believing that the Army will lose an indifferent infantryman and gain a first rate cavalryman.

He is a first rate horseman and will undoubtedly keep himself well mounted.

Very respectfully, Colonel
Your obb. ser
/s/ J. L. Kemper
Maj. Gen.

Private Goss was transferred to the cavalry and served honorably to the end of the war.[32]

Kemper was also active socially. He was the last person to visit William Lennow Kirkland, a wealthy South Carolina planter and volunteer aide to General R.S. Ripley, who had been wounded and was on his death bed. Mary Chestnut recorded in her diary, "General Kemper saw poor Kirkland," who died the next day.[33]

The War was not going well for the Confederacy. Lee's army was in the trenches at Petersburg and facing heavy losses from battlefield casualties, disease and desertion. Losses in the ranks were filled with

32. Maria William Minor *The Walkers of Woodberry Forest* (n.c., 1973), p. 92.
33. C. Vann Woodward, ed. *Mary Chestnut's Civil War* (New Haven, 1981), p. 618.

Kemper's reserves, leaving only old men, boys and invalids available to guard bridges and warehouses and do sentry duty at the White House and government offices. Yankee intelligence had learned of this precarious condition, prompting General Ulysses S. Grant to remark, "They are now robbing the cradle and the grave."[34]

No matter how desperate things looked, Kemper remained optimistic. In January 1865 he advocated wholesale impressment of supplies to replenish the army.[35] On February 7, 1865, General John Cabell Breckenridge was sworn in as the Secretary of War to replace James Seddon, who had just resigned. Kemper was mentioned to possibly head the Bureau of War.[36]

Also in February, Kemper urged acceptance of one of the most drastic proposals ever heard in the Confederacy—the emancipation of all slaves and issuance of a proclamation stating that the Confederacy was fighting only for the right of self-government and independence and not for preservation of slavery.[37] After much debate the Confederate Congress passed an act granting freedom to all slaves who enlisted in the Confederate army, and soon regiments of black troops were being drilled and readied for battle.

Kemper was given absolute control over the conscription service on March 7th, although Colonel John S. Preston, who had up until this time served as head of the Bureau of Conscription, violently disagreed with the decision to place Kemper in charge.[38] Kemper was extremely effective in this position, but by this late date there was little anyone could do to save the Confederate States of America from collapse.

---

34. Clifford Dowdey *The Land They Fought For: The Story of the South as the Confederacy 1832-1865* (Garden City, New Jersey, 1955), p. 388.
35. Jones, "Forgotten Virginian," p. 319.
36. Younger, p. 199.
37. Jones, "Forgotten Virginian," p. 319.
38. *Ibid.*, pp. 317-318.

Chapter 20

The Last Days of the Confederacy

Early April of 1865 found Kemper still actively working on new ways to increase the reserve forces of Virginia in his effort to help General Lee survive the battering onslaught of Grant's forces around Petersburg and Richmond. Kemper was still optimistic of eventual Confederate success,[1] but despite his optimism and hard work the tide was turning against the Confederacy. On Sunday afternoon, April 2nd, Lee ordered the evacuation of Petersburg. By nightfall, the Confederate Army of Northern Virginia was in full retreat toward Lynchburg. The capital city of Richmond was no longer tenable, and President Davis, his cabinet, and the Confederate government fled by rail the same night. Communications between President Davis and Lee's army were disrupted, and the Confederate government was poised on the brink of of collapse.

Kemper, as commander of the state's reserve forces, director of the conscription service and commander of the local defenses of Richmond, was in a state of confusion as he watched his country fall apart before his very eyes. General Ewell, who had been Kemper's immediate superior officer, was nowhere to be found and Kemper wandered from office to office at the War Department

---

1. Jones "Conservative Virginian," p. 1.

looking for someone to apply to for orders.[2] Kemper was subsequently ordered to leave Richmond; he had no part in the evacuation and burning of the city that took place upon the withdrawal of the last Confederate troops.[3]

As Lee's weary army trudged westward in forlorn hopes of uniting forces with General Johnston's army in North Carolina, they fought a series of sharp, desperate skirmishes. Kemper had no part in these final battles of the war, but went directly to Danville, which had been named the provisional capital of the Confederate States of America. There President Davis and the governmental officials attempted to maintain some semblance of civil authority.

The top officials of the Commonwealth of Virginia had fled the capital, leaving the state without any civil government. The General Assembly at its last meeting on April 2nd had voted to reconvene the state government at Lynchburg, but that didn't happen, and the governor, William "Extra-Billy" Smith, was in hiding in Rockbridge County with a $25,000 bounty on his head.

General Lee surrendered to General Grant on April 9, 1865, at Appomattox Court House. Grant's policy of attrition had exhausted Confederate manpower and resources. Kemper was disappointed at the final outcome, but couldn't stifle a deep feeling of relief, as well. It had been a long, hard war, and he had suffered greatly. He believed the words of Lincoln's second inaugural address, "with malice toward none, with charity for all," and regarded the president's statements as a magnanimous assurance that the South would be welcomed back as equal and honorable men.[4] Kemper

---

2.   A.A. Hoehling and Mary Hoehling *The Last Days of the Confederacy: An Eyewitness Account of the Fall of Richmond, Capitol City of the Confederate States* (New York, 1981), p. 127; J. B. Jones *A Rebel War Clerk's Diary at the Confederate States Capitol* (Philadelphia, 1866), vol. II, pp. 465-466.

3.   Jones, "Conservative Virginian," p. 2.

4.   Kemper papers V.H.S.

wanted to do what was right. He felt that the Southerners had "surrendered in good and knightly faith, devoutly intending to be faithful and law-abiding citizens under and of, what was thereafter to be, our government and country—our country—the only country left us."[5]

Following Lee's surrender, President Davis and what was left of Confederate civil authority continued their flight southward over war-torn roads and damaged rail lines that made travel extremely difficult. Since Kemper's wound had not healed completely, and a persistent, throbbing pain left him unable to endure a long journey on horseback, he surrendered to the union forces at Danville.

He was paroled on May 2nd by order of Major General Horatio Gouveneur Wright, the commander of the union VI Corps.

Kemper's family had spent the last chaotic months of the war in Halifax County, far removed from the fighting and close to his sister, Sarah Bocock, and her family.[6] He appealed to Wright's provost marshal, Major D.H. Miles, to guarantee their safe passage back home. Miles issued a safe-conduct authorization: "[A]ll Guards and Patrols will permit him to pass to his home in Madison Cty. Va. and will permit him to take his family and effects with him and will see that he is not molested or interfered with."[7] An additional order was issued protecting Kemper's property from "stragglers" and union "foraging parties."[8]

From Danville Kemper went to Richmond, where he spent a considerable amount of time keeping in touch with the latest developments in military and political matters, then moved his family back to Madison Court House and re-established their residence there.[9]

Kemper earnestly believed in the righteousness of the Southern

5. *Ibid.*
6. Jones "Conservative Virginian," pp. 6-7.
7. Kemper papers U.Va.
8. *Ibid.*
9. Jones "Conservative Virginian," p. 7.

Cause, and he had given his all for the Confederacy. He best explained the motives that had inspired him and other Southerners to go to war and continue the fight until all of their new nation's resources were exhausted in a letter to a correspondent in the North some years after the war:

> You and we differed as to the nature of the Government, and in 1861 we drew the sword in what we believed and still believe was as holy a cause as ever inspired a people with deliberate valor. We gave $3,000,000,000 of wealth to that cause. We lavished our best blood upon it. Were we insincere, or wicked, or criminals? When I was shot to pieces in scaling your breastworks at Gettysburg, under the muzzles of your guns, was I impelled by no higher motive than animates a penitentiary thief? Be convinced, Sir, that a man who pours out his blood for a cause, exhibits a lofty and sacred devotion to principle which characterizes none but noble minds, and which, even if it were prompted by error of judgment or education ought to command the respect of all honorable men.[10]

---

10.   Kemper papers V.H.S., letter of August 22, 1868.

Chapter 21

Beginning Anew

When the Kempers returned to Madison Court House, they had to start life anew, and the immediate future looked bleak. Their home had been burned by raiding Yankees, their savings were gone, having been invested in now-worthless Confederate bonds, and the money owed to them was uncollectible.[1] On top of all that, Kemper suffered the effects of the terrible wound that would greatly curtail his activities for the rest of his life.

Kemper's position in the post-war socio-economic order was very difficult. Like most returning Confederates, he had large debts, no savings and, due to the collapse of the South's financial institutions, no way of borrowing. He had sacrificed his all for the Southern Cause and was left beggared by the War. He owed his creditors between $8,000 and $10,000, which he could have paid his debts had he been able to collect on debts owed to him. The financial ruin of his debtors, and the debtor laws passed by the state, prevented the collection of many of these debts. Kemper could have used the debtor and bankruptcy laws to his own advantage, but he considered the payment of a debt a moral obligation and refused to benefit by such laws.[2]

---

1. Jones "Conservative Virginian," p. 13.
2. *Ibid.*, p. 12.

Armed with a loving family, a fine political and military reputation, and a determination to succeed, Kemper set about rebuilding their life. The family sought immediate refuge with Belle's parents, crowding in on Belfield and Cremora Cave, whose home had survived the conflict. Kemper tried rebuild his law practice, but many of his pre-war clients were now unable to pay.

Madison County, like the rest of the South, had suffered from the war. Formerly well-to-do men were now reduced to virtual poverty. Farms were in ruins, and few factories or mills were still operating. Greeting the homeward bound soldiers were miles of broken fences, solitary chimneys, and the charred ruins of their homes. Twenty of the county's churches had been burned, and the labor system was disrupted. Land values had plunged from $150 per acre before the war to just $2 an acre in 1865.[3]

In addition to his other problems, Kemper was concernced with his wife's health. Belle had never been physically strong and now, pained with the mental anguish of the war, the death of her daughter and the wounding of her husband, her fragile condition worsened. In 1865, she was stricken by an eye infection. Despite the efforts of expensive specialists in Richmond, Belle would never be able to see well again, and in a few years she would be completely blind.[4]

In August 1865, Cremora Cave bought a house on a five-acre lot in the town of Madison for her daughter and son-in-law and their family. In 1868, Kemper bought out his mother-in-law's share of the house for $3,000.[5]

The house, still standing, is a Greek Revival style ante-bellum frame structure with an Ionic columned front porch, a hipped roof and two floors above the English basement, built circa 1852 for state senator Thomas N. Welch. The house sits on a high ridge just

---

3.   Woodward, *For Home and Honor*, p. 88.
4.   Jones "Conservative Virginian," p. 11.
5.   *Ibid.*, p. 13.

118

east of and overlooking today's Main Street (the old Blue Ridge Turnpike.) There were a number of outside dependencies including a kitchen, smokehouse, servants' quarters, carriage shed/granary and a small frame building used by Kemper as a law office.[6]

Kemper contributed to the support of his elderly mother and widowed sister, Susan E. Matthews, while struggling to support his own family. He served as attorney for his brother John, who also lost nearly everything he owned during the war. Kemper also kept in close contact with his brother Frederick, who ran a school in Missouri, and his sister, Mary A. Freeman, who lived nearby in Gordonsville.[7]

A practical problem facing Kemper and other former slave owners was their relationship with their former slaves. As a result of their emancipation, the ex-slaves were forced into a lifestyle for which they were ill-prepared and for quite some time relations between the races were extremely strained. Economically, the abolishment of slavery resulted in the loss to the former owners of the slaves as taxable property. The difficulty of getting good labor as a result of the newly freed slaves' change in status was detrimental to the labor system and necessitated serious adjustments. Belle once remarked to her sister-in-law that the "darky question" was causing a good deal of concern in the Madison area. Jails were overcrowded with Negroes who had committed a multitude of petty crimes.[8]

Unfortunately for all Southerners, President Lincoln's plans for a quick, reasonable readjustment were not implemented. The South was in for a long, hard period of reconstruction. President Andrew Johnson appointed Francis H. Pierpoint as governor of Virginia. Pierpoint intended to provide for a truly representative General Assembly, but once the election was held, the radical majority in

---

6.   The author is project manager of the Kemper Mansion Restoration.

7.   Jones "Conservative Virginian," p. 14.

8.   *Ibid.*, p. 16.

Congress blocked them from taking their seats. All former Confederate officials and political leaders were forbidden to hold office and denied the right to vote.[9]

President Johnson issued a Proclamation of Pardon on May 29, 1865, which excluded the benefits of general pardons, including the right to vote and hold office, to thirteen categories of Confederate officers, officials, and supporters. Those exempt from a general pardon could petition the president for special clemency.[10]

This amounted to a great deal of red tape, time and trouble for former Confederates. Some, such as former-governor "Extra-Billy" Smith were loathe to cooperate with the military authorities and the radical state government. Kemper, however, saw the wisdom of co-operating with the authorities. In the summer of 1865 he helped organize a meeting of the people of Madison County to "take in consideration the state of the county." Recognizing the results of, and accepting the existing situation, the meeting passed a political resolution in which they discounted as "unwise and improper, any further resistance to the Government of the United States." They promised in good faith and to the extent of their ability "to cooperate with Governor Pierpoint in securing peace and order in preserving Christian civilization, and restoring the material prosperity of Virginia."[11]

The meeting appointed a committee of five county leaders. Kemper, former general Robert A. Banks and attorney William O. Fry were three of those chosen to "wait upon Governor Pierpoint with the forgoing Resolution and confer with him as to the best means of giving effect thereto." The delegation met favorably with the governor, who discussed at some length with Kemper the re-establishment of local government and the policies of the state

---

9.   *Ibid.*, pp. 19-20.
10.   *Ibid.*, p. 20.
11.   Woodward *For Home and Honor*, p. 91.

120

government.[12] Pierpoint recognized the desirability of Kemper's proposals, but because of the radicals in power, he was unable to do anything to bring about a satisfactory solution to the problems.

To further complicate matters, Robert E. Lee and Jefferson Davis, among others, were indicted for treason. This action brought about a great deal of bitterness and disappointment. Most former Confederates waited to see what Lee would do before taking any action. When Lee took the amnesty oath and sought a pardon, most followed his lead and did likewise.[13]

Kemper filed a petition for pardon and for the restoration of his rights on July 1, 1865, one month after Lee. In the petition, Kemper spoke of himself in the third person, "He petitions that he may resume the duties and privileges of a citizen of the United States and be permitted to exercise and enjoy the same in *bona fide* compliance with, and subordination to, the Constitution and laws of the country."[14] The next week Kemper traveled to Richmond, where he swore before a notary public that the facts in his petition were true. He also secured the endorsement of Governor Pierpoint. All of the paperwork was then delivered to former Confederate brigadier general Patrick T. Moore, an Irish immigrant who had served under Kemper in 1864 in the Virginia reserves, who had begun operating of a "pardoning agency" in Richmond.[15]

In late August, he signed the formal, printed amnesty oath to support the federal constitution and accept the emancipation of the slaves. He also sought additional support for his petition and on October 23, 1865, it was accepted by President Johnson. Kemper was granted a "full pardon and amnesty."[16]

---

12.   *Ibid.*, p. 91; Jones "Conservative Virginian," p. 22.
13.   Lee was finally pardoned and his citizenship restored on August 5, 1975, during the administration of President Gerald Ford.
14.   Amnesty papers, National Archives.
15.   Jones "Conservative Virginian," p. 25.
16.   *Ibid.*, pp. 26-27.

Kemper was held in contempt by the unreconstructed rebels led by former governor and general, Henry A. Wise. In a letter to Wise, Kemper hotly defended his action:

When after the war, I found myself under the ban of a special proscription, duress and tyranny, I followed the example and personal counsel of General Lee, in addressing a manful and intrepid appeal to the same government, not to pardon any act of my life, but to restore me to whatever rights of citizenship were left the body of our people, in order that going down with them in a common overthrow, I might the more effectively struggle with them for political and material restoration. Never have I failed to negate all ideas of repenting ought of my past. Never have I failed to guard as the pride and glory of my life, my service as a Confederate soldier. Let me tell you I know a thousand-fold more than you ever knew of General Lee and of what he did and thought in this connection.[17]

---

17.   Kemper papers U.Va., Kemper to Henry A. Wise, August 30, 1873.

Chapter 22

Business Ventures

For Kemper and other Confederate attorneys, the opportunity for a post-war legal vocation looked bleak. The state was occupied by federal troops, and the military courts and tribunals of the Freedman's Bureau took the place of civilian courts. Since it was impossible to make a living in his chosen profession, Kemper had to look to other areas to provide for his family.

Kemper had very definite ideas about Virginia's future, strongly believing that the Old Dominion's lands, forests, minerals and manufacturing must be developed. He was a staunch supporter of expansion of the state's railroads and believed in the acquisition of badly needed labor and capital from outside the state.

Kemper's first business venture following the war was undertaken in late July 1865. He joined Patrick T. Moore in his profitable pardoning business, handling pardons in Madison and surrounding counties for fees ranging from $300 to $500. He felt this work was valuable and that for its honest performance he should be adequately rewarded. He processed several pardons for former Confederates in the Madison area, including those of his good friends Robert Adam Banks, B.T.F. Conway, and T.S. Conway.[1]

In late September, Michael Harman of Staunton called together a group of former Confederates to organize and incorporate the National Express and Transportation Company. Kemper touted the company as "the greatest company in the world" and assured friends that it would "furnish employment for the officers and men who are survivors of our late army." He was urged to take an active part and a good paying position with the company.[2]

The company was, in effect, an outgrowth of the old Southern Express Company which had been incorporated in Virginia in 1861. This expanded project was to operate throughout Virginia and the South. It was conceived and promoted by Harman and Richmond bankers Charles W. Purcell and L.W. Glazebrook. Joseph E. Johnston was elected president at the organizational meeting in Richmond. The board of directors consisted of Harmon, Purcell, Glazebrook, John Echols of Staunton and New York businessman Benjamin Hart. John D. Imboden was chosen as general superintendent and Kemper was elected treasurer. Others involved in the company were Patrick Moore, Thomas L. Rosser, and John Dooley, all former Confederates. Before the end of November, the company had set up corporate headquarters at Richmond and Kemper had an office there. As the company grew, its agents covered a wide area including New York, Ohio, South Carolina and Georgia. The company received requests from all across the South for jobs and positions.[3]

On December 12, 1865, the National Express and Transportation Company was incorporated in Virginia to "do an express and general transportation business, by land and by water, for the conveyance of persons and property of every kind throughout or beyond the limits of Virginia." Actually, the company's main

1.　　Jones "Conservative Virginian," pp. 31-33.
2.　　Kemper papers U.Va.
3.　　Jones "Conservative Virginian," pp. 33-35.

124

business was the quick transportation of small parcels, money orders and letters. The capital stock of the company was fixed at $5,000,000. Shares were sold at $100 each. The stock sold well and the company was off to a good start, although it faced stiff competition from older, well-established companies such as the Adams Express Company and from the railroads.[4]

In early February, Imboden became the company's chief legal counsel, and Kemper replaced him as general superintendent. In April, Kemper quit active participation in the company's affairs and left his office in Richmond, however he remained involved in the company until 1885.[5]

In October, Kemper became co-agent with Walter Harrison in attracting business connections in New York to speculate in southern lands and move into the southern labor and capital market. The American Industrial Agency opened a Richmond branch and offered Kemper the position of president.

Kemper also was an agent for the New York Southern Lands Company. Also with the company were Joseph R. Anderson of the Tredegar Iron Works in Richmond and Catesby ap. R. Jones (C.S.N.) as vice president. Kemper showed a great deal of interest in these Northern business concerns.[6]

Kemper actively promoted the idea of a corporate company funded by large capital raised in England to restore the agricultural system of the Tidewater and Piedmont areas of Virginia. He saw the solution to the state's labor problem in the immigration of large numbers of English laborers. The top echelon of the company was to be former high-ranking Confederate officers. He sought the support of John Tyler, Jr., William H. Payne, Seth M. Barton, and Sidney D. Jackman, but these plans failed to materialize.[7]

---

4. *Ibid.*, p. 36.
5. *Ibid.*, p. 37.
6. *Ibid.*, p. 40.
7. *Ibid.*, pp. 40-41.

Kemper also had plans to develop the numerous mineral deposits in Madison County. In 1868 Kemper advertised, "for speculation and sale, mines of gold, silver, copper, and corundum, within 20 miles of Madison C.H. . . . pronounced by the ablest experts to be incalculably rich." The most important of these were the copper deposits on the Middle River property of his clients Edwin Booton and a Mr. Cole.[8]

Kemper was the agent of both men for the sale of their copper. Barton helped Kemper promote these lands with promotional literature and elaborate plans to pursue domestic and foreign markets. Kemper was assured that these were the "richest—easiest worked and most accessible copper mines in the world." They were believed to hold millions of dollars worth of copper. It was, however, extremely difficult to market the property. Kemper found most Yankee speculators to be unscrupulous, and although he worked hard and continued his efforts as late as 1872, little interest materialized.[9]

Kemper maintained an interest in the field of mineral resource development despite this disappointing and unsuccessful venture. He also actively sought a position in the railroads, which he saw as the key industry in Virginia. He sought the presidency of the Orange and Alexandria Railroad, actively soliciting his friends in the legislature to help him secure the position. His leading opponent, John S. Barbour, Jr., the brother of his old friend, James Barbour, was elected president over Kemper and led the railroad for the next two decades.[10]

Despite several less than successful ventures, Kemper continued to advocate northern and foreign investment in the South. He expressed rather frankly his attitudes and thoughts in a letter to a New York correspondent:

Do you suppose we are so cursed with judicial blindness as to

---

8.   *Ibid.*, p. 42.
9.   *Ibid.*, pp. 43-44.
10.   *Ibid.*, p. 48.

prefer poverty to wealth, as to shut out the capital and labor which alone are wanting to make this magnificent state the Eldorado of the South? . . . I do, and the whole mass of Southern white men sincerely desire . . . men who come from whatever quarter to abide here as citizens and honestly share our fortunes. [They] are welcomed with universal and heart-felt cordiality. We desire and invite you to come and purchase our lands from $2 to $30 per acre, which in the harsher climate of New York would command from $40 to $600 per acre. I shall call upon any decent, *bona fide* immigrant who comes to my vicinity from the North and tender him the courtesies and offices of good neighborhood, without knowing or caring for his previous political affiliations.[11]

He went on to describe the rich mineral lands he held for operation and for sale. Kemper challenged him to visit the South if he still doubted that Southerners favored the development of a more diversified and balanced economy. Although a newcomer (like most Southerners) to the varied economic activities they engaged in after the war, Kemper proved to be extraordinarily energetic and efficient. Although inexperienced, he was somewhat successful and very optimistic, if perhaps a little naive.

---

11.   Kemper papers V.H.S., Kemper to William A. Baker, August 22, 1868.

Chapter 23

The Country Lawyer Resumes His Practice

By the end of 1865, civil courts were allowed to resume their former jurisdiction and Kemper decided to renew his law practice. He considered opening an office in Richmond, but finally elected to stay in Madison and practice law from the small office behind his home.

Debt collection and its attendant lawsuits made up a large portion of his legal business. The General Assembly, unfortunately, passed a bill to stay the collection of debts until 1868. This, combined with homestead provisions, caused Kemper's legal practice to suffer.

It was a rough time for a small town lawyer. Because of the scarcity of funds, Kemper was forced to accept bartered items in payment for services. The disrupted mail system hampered legal commerce, and the disappearance and post-war disarray of legal papers and court records created other problems for Southern lawyers.

The roads had suffered greatly from military use and destruction during the war, making travel difficult. Kemper spent a great deal of time traveling over the bad roads and, because of his old wound, such travel was especially hard on him. In a letter to a friend, he reported, "I have just got home after riding nearly all night after an absence of about a week. I have been in the mountains of Greene [County], riding in all the late rains with a Baltimore merchant on urgent business. And am just now getting home half-dead with fatigue."[1]

Things were so bad that Kemper even considered emigrating to a foreign country, possibly Mexico.[2]

Gradually, however, his law practice began to pick up and his income improved. Drawing up deeds and contracts kept him busy, and before long he was again handling cases in Madison and the surrounding counties. In 1866 he formed a partnership with William O. Fry.[3] He also formed a partnership with his old friend in the Valley, John Imboden.[4]

Kemper frequently corresponded with General George Stoneman concerning the United States military's interference in legal matters in Virginia. In 1867 the United States Congress passed the bankruptcy laws, and Kemper traveled to Alexandria to qualify as an "attorney and counselor of the Circuit Court of the United States in and for the District of Virginia." Before long he was doing a considerable business in bankruptcy cases.

Kemper built up a fine reputation as a civil and criminal lawyer. He handled cases of all sorts, including the acceptance of Confederate money in payment of debts, claims against the federal government for confiscation of forage, and settlement of estates, as well as a large number of criminal cases that included murders and assaults. His clients were both colored and white, rich and poor. He received a great deal of correspondence from all over the country and handled some out-of-state cases. He commanded much respect for his integrity, honesty, and thorough knowledge of the law and wielded a great deal of influence. He was a good business man, ef-

---

1. Kemper papers U.Va. August 18, 1872.
2. Jones "Conservative Virginian," p. 61.
3. *Ibid.*, p. 62.
4. *Ibid.*, pp. 63-64.

ficient and prompt. In the court room, he was passionate, often literary, forceful, logical and known for his oratory.[5]

His fees ranged from $5 to $50 for routine cases, up to $500 for more complicated matters. As his financial situation improved, he purchased land, some for his own use, some for speculation. He bought half-interest in 419 acres on the James River in Cumberland County, and on his own bought the Kinderhook farm of several hundred acres on Middle River in Madison County and 266 acres of the richest farmland in the county on White Oak Run in Hebron Valley.[6]

Kemper had enjoyed farming since his childhood days on the plantation and sought a return to the pre-war planter-class life. He had a deep concern for the future of agriculture and development of agricultural resources. For his own farming operation he procured the best implements available and used only the most highly regarded fertilizers and seeds. His chief crops were small grains: wheat, corn and oats. He owned a few fine horses and several draft horses.

He ordered products such as flour, sugar, coffee, tea, and fine tobacco from firms in Richmond, Culpeper and Gordonsville. His suits were tailor-made in Richmond. He took great pride in his gardens and was a regular patron of the state's finest tree nurseries. Strong spirits, especially the brandy and whiskey for which he had a fondness, were ordered in large quantities, often by the barrel.[7]

Kemper realized the value of a good education for his children and those of the community. His son Meade attended the Locust Dale Academy. In the spring of 1868, he saw the need for easily available education facilities in Madison County, founded the Madison Academy, and hired A.D. Armistead of Matthews County as schoolmaster. The academy was small and offered a varied cur-

---

5.   *Ibid.*, pp. 65-66.
6.   *Ibid.*, pp. 69-71.
7.   *Ibid.*, pp. 72-74.

riculum of liberal arts, ancient languages, English, mathematics and modern languages to both boys and girls. He sought pupils with advertisements and personally served as treasurer and general sponsor with the help of Dr. J.W. Taylor and William E. Banks. Meade and Florence Kemper attended the academy, along with children of thirteen other area families.[8]

In 1870, tragedy again struck the family. Belle Kemper fell seriously ill in the spring. Her condition improved considerably, but in late summer she fell ill again, her situation complicated by a pregnancy. On September 8th she gave birth to a son, Reginald Heber Johns. The birth proved too great a strain in her weakened condition, and in less than a month Belle Kemper was dead at age 33.

Belle had been pretty, friendly, and vivacious. Her death was both tragic and shocking, a severe blow to Kemper. He was an intense, high strung man, and Belle was his only love, his sweetheart from youth. For months after her passing he did little but dream of how as a young man he had won the hand of a beautiful young girl still in her teens. He wrote:

I saw a man whose brow was pale as marble—whose eyes dilated and whose lips trembled from emotions stronger than he could utter. . . . He held in an impassioned grief the hand of a girl just budding luxuriantly into earliest womanhood. It was not her unwonted precision or symmetry of feature that made her beautiful; her *features* were not seen at all. They were thrown out of view—suffused—beaming—with a glow which was sent mantling to her countenance by the intense throbbing of her heart. . . . She more than fulfilled his ideal in everything—grew brighter from every trial—and proved to be gold in the crucible. Time passed on and I saw other scenes.[9]

8.　　*Ibid.*, pp. 74-76.
9.　　Kemper papers U.Va., Kemper to Cremora Cave, December 28, 1870.

Belle's death left him broken in health, in energy, and in spirits. He moved out of the house to be alone with his grief and took up residence in his law office, calling it his sleeping room. There, beneath portraits of Robert E. Lee and Stonewall Jackson, Kemper dealt with his misfortune. [10]

Eventually Kemper was able to control his memories, busy himself with hard work and concentrate on the future, but he never forgot his beloved wife, and he never remarried.

10.   *Ibid.*, Kemper to C. W. Purcell, February 10, 1870.

Chapter 24

Return to Politics

Like the other disenfranchised Confederates, Kemper could not vote in the 1865 election, but he supported the conservative Alexander H.H. Stuart of Staunton for the United States House of Representatives. On September 8th, Stuart was Kemper's guest at a political rally in Madison Court House.[1]

In December, when the Radicals refused admission to the halls of Congress to the representatives of the South, including Stuart, Southerners realized that something had to be done to restore self government to the majority. Kemper felt that the South must "raise up our bleeding country from the dust and set her free."[2]

Most Southerners were afraid that the very foundation of our nation would be eroded by a strong centralized government, believing that a concentration of powers would increase the dangers of political absolutism and tyranny. Kemper wrote, "In modern times the tendency to a centralization of the power of government has almost everywhere irresistibly borne down every impediment to its progress."[3]

About this time Kemper became acquainted with an English war

1.   Kemper papers U.Va.
2.   *Ibid.*
3.   Kemper papers V.H.S.

correspondent, M. Butt Hewson, who had covered the war in the South and was very sympathetic to southern views. Together, Kemper and Hewson advocated the founding of a weekly journal, called *The States,* to present southern views and desires. One former Confederate general from each southern state was to be responsible for getting 1,000 subscribers in his respective state and to raise support through contributions and advertising sales.

Besides Kemper in Virginia, participants included A.R. Wright from Georgia, Benjamin G. Humphreys from Mississippi, Robert F. Hoke from North Carolina, Charles W. Field from Kentucky, Basil Duke from Kentucky, Alexander H. Stephens and Howell Cobb of Georgia, R.M.T. Hunter of Virginia, and John Bell of Tennessee.[4]

Former United States presidents Franklin Pierce and Millard Fillmore also showed interest in the paper, but despite a great deal of discussion, the paper was never published.[5]

About this time the new Freedman's Bureau bill and the Civil Rights Act were passed by Congress, giving Negroes suffrage and citizenship and causing a great deal of concern among white Southerners.

Early in 1867, state delegate A.W. Graves of Madison spearheaded a movement to nominate the popular Kemper for governor. Among his leading supporters were delegates John Goode of Norfolk, A.G. Pendleton of Giles, J.C. Woodson of Rockingham, C.W.C. Dunnington of Prince William, former general William H. Richardson, state senator Dale Carter of Russell, and former senator Thomas Welch.[6]

The legislature was split along old party lines with the Whigs supporting John B. Baldwin of Augusta County and the Democrats supporting Kemper. In February, Kemper went to Richmond to talk

---

4.   Jones "Conservative Virginian," p. 86.
5.   *Ibid,* p. 87; Kemper papers U.Va.
6.   *Ibid,* pp. 91-92.

with friends about his candidacy. No less than eighteen persons had expressed an interest in running for governor, with Kemper the forerunner.

On March 2, 1867, the United States Congress passed the Reconstruction Act, creating Military District I of what used to be the commonwealth of Virginia. With the state under martial law, no election was held. Instead, General John M. Schofield was appointed commander of the military district. Since ex-Confederates were disenfranchised by the act, only Negroes and carpetbaggers could vote, thereby putting the Radicals in power in the state.[7]

This action forced the ex-Confederates to redouble their efforts to regain their suffrage. Their immediate goal was to register all white men who were still eligible to vote.

In June, Kemper addressed the alumni of his alma mater, Washington College in Lexington. He delivered a lengthy address concerning the political situation of the time in which he defended secession but also urged better relations with the North and the federal government.[8]

Kemper's reasonable and moderate view of civil rights was rare among white Southerners of the time. He recognized Negroes as human beings and felt they should be given the same basic human rights as whites.

The white conservatives failed to organize effectively and the election of 1867 was an overwhelming victory for the Radical Party. Seventy-two Radicals, twenty-five of them Negroes, were elected to the state's constitutional convention, more than double the number of conservatives elected.[9] Madison County elected conservative Robert S. Beazley, so the Madison County conservatives

---

7. *Ibid*, p. 94.
8. *Ibid*, p. 100; Allen W. Moger *Virginia: Bourbonism to Byrd 1870-1925* (Charlottesville, 1968), p. 21; Kemper papers U.Va.
9. *Ibid*, p. 102.

fared far better than their counterparts in the rest of the state.[10]

Given their resounding defeat, the conservatives recognized the need for better organization and called for a statewide convention. Counties and cities were urged to send delegates to the convention held in Richmond on December 11 and 12. Delegates included: Alexander H.H. Stuart, John Letcher, R.M.T. Hunter, Thomas S. Bocock, James B. Baldwin, R.T. Daniel, James Barbour, Thomas S. Flournoy, John Randolph Tucker, and Thomas Jefferson Randolph, some of the most influential men in the state at the time. Delegates from Madison County were: Kemper, Thomas P. Wallace, A.W. Graves, Robert A. Banks, and Thomas Smoot.[11]

Stuart was elected president of the new Conservative Party of Virginia and Kemper was elected one of nine vice-presidents. Although opposing rule by the Negroes, the party adopted a resolution declaring their acceptance of the abolition of slavery. They also declared the impracticality of secession, urged quick restoration of the Union and the return of peace, unity and good will. They asked that Virginians be extended all rights and privileges guaranteed American citizens by the constitution.[12] Kemper served with Letcher and Baldwin on the committee for the sixth congressional district.[13]

Virginia was entering a transitional period. The men of the new Conservative Party would play a major role in this transition, and James Lawson Kemper would play a major role in his new party.

---

10. *Ibid*, p. 105.
11. *Ibid*, pp. 106-107.
12. *Ibid*, p. 108.
13. *Ibid*, p. 108.

Chapter 25

The Conservatives Become Effective

After the War Between the States, the overwhelming majority of Virginians still lived on farms, and the economy of the commonwealth was still agriculturally oriented, but war and depression had stripped away the antebellum prosperity from the land, revealing a grim reality of poverty and decay, a desolate countryside with thousands of acres of gullied fields of broom-sedge wilderness. Once-fertile fields were covered with scrub oaks and stunted pines, the landscape dotted with decayed fences, half-starved cattle, ramshackle houses and the remnants of crumbling mansions.

The post-war years brought deflated agricultural prices, high interest rates and burdensome taxes. There was stiff competition from the agriculturally rich prairies of the west, and a harsh weather pattern brought ruinous droughts, voracious insects and early frosts. Wages for blacks and whites declined to $5 to $10 per month. Agricultural laborers, tenant farmers and sharecroppers faced endless poverty and debt. Illiteracy plagued 20 per cent of the white population and nearly 75 per cent of the Negroes.

The Tidewater area was devastated by the collapse of the pre-war plantation system. Truck farms with their crops of peanuts, corn and potatoes replaced huge tobacco and cotton plantations. The fishing industry prospered; oystermen in small boats made cities like Norfolk and Suffolk bustle with activity. The mountain counties were different. They had been less dependent on slave labor and few Negroes lived there. That region of the state was rich in coal and iron deposits. Heavy industry was practically non-existent in the state.

Members of the former wealthy planter class moved to the cities and sought careers in urban commerce or the learned professions. The state was linked to northern cities and markets by rail and telegraph. Towns connected by rail saw new life as economic, social, and political centers. Merchants, hostlers, blacksmiths, and other small businessmen became the new community leaders. County fairs and court days were the leading social functions, and weekly newspapers kept the citizenry informed.

The small towns that served as county seats in Virginia were all similar. Each had unpaved streets which were dusty in drought and muddy in rain, no sidewalks, inadequate or non-existent sewer and water systems, shanties on the outskirts, stray dogs, gambling dens and saloons. There were a few larger, more prosperous exceptions. Lynchburg, Danville, and Staunton benefitted from the prosperity of the tobacco industry and railroad construction. These towns were noted for their attractive buildings.[1]

Before the war Virginia had spent millions on internal improvements, and the state was a substantial stockholder in many private railroads, canals, and turnpikes. During the war the state had lost one-third of its land area by the secession of West Virginia, the state's public works were in ruin, and the people were plundered, impoverished, and subdued.[2] After four years of fighting, death, and destruction, Virginians knew what it was like to lose a war. One Virginia newspaper editor remarked, "Our hopes have fled,

---

1.   James Tice Moore *Two Paths to the New South: The Virginia Debt Controversy 1870-1883* (Lexington, Kentucky, 1974), pp. 1-10.
2.   *Ibid.*, p. 5.

and we sit in darkness."[3]

As the commander of the military occupation, General Schofield supervised the registration of voters and prepared a convention to draw up a new constitution. Since the majority of voters were Negroes, the constitution would be prepared by Radicals. A New York native, John C. Underwood, was selected president of the convention.[4]

The Radical Party was comprised chiefly of Negroes and led by carpetbaggers and scalawags. The resulting constitution allowed Radical domination of state government and was opposed by all of the state's Conservatives.

The Conservative Party was comprised of former Democrats, Whigs, and Know-Nothings. Bankers, merchants, lawyers, doctors and the remnants of the old planter class joined together. The leaders cherished the memory of the old aristocratic order and believed the state should be led by Virginia's elite.

Kemper saw the Conservative Party as one to "inaugurate a new era . . . when men of both races combining for the good of all, would restore peace, and a common prosperity." The party emphasized states' rights and opposed the centralization of government power. Kemper led the party in Madison County. He vigorously rallied the people of Madison in opposition to the Underwood constitution.[5]

In May the Conservative state committee met in Richmond to choose candidates for state office in case the Underwood constitution was ratified. Robert E. Withers of Lynchburg was nominated for governor; James A. Walker of Pulaski for lieutenant governor; and John L. Marye, Jr., of Fredericksburg for attorney general.[6] Kemper did some campaigning in Madison for the Conservative

---

3. Moger, p. 4.
4. *Ibid.*, p. 6.
5. Jones, "Conservative Virginian," pp. 109-113.
6. *Ibid.*, p. 114.

ticket, but the ratification vote was postponed indefinitely by the military authorities.

Kemper manifested a deep interest in the presidential campaign of 1868 and served as delegate to the national Democratic convention in New York on July 4th, along with James Barbour, T.S. Bocock and John B. Baldwin. They hoped the national party would take a strong stand against the Radicals.[7]

Kemper supported Francis P. Blair of Missouri, but Horatio Seymour, the former governor of New York, was nominated for president, with Blair as vice president. Ulysses S. Grant, the Republican candidate, was elected.[8]

Alexander H.H. Stuart stepped into the political picture and launched a "New Movement" to get Virginia re-admitted to the Union as quickly as possible. He organized a meeting of prominent Conservatives to form a strategy and led a Committee of Nine that went to Washington and called on President Grant and Congress. Kemper strongly supported Stuart.[9] Their efforts were successful, and on April 10th the Congress, with the recommendations of Grant, provided for Virginia's restoration. The military commander set July 6th for elections to vote for state offices, congress, and ratification of the constitution.[10]

At this time a newcomer to state politics entered the picture, William Mahone. Mahone hoped to influence the elections with his money and power as president of three railroads, the Norfolk and Petersburg, the Southside, and the Virginia and Tennessee. A wealthy, self-made man, Mahone would play an important role in Virginia politics for years to come.

Mahone wanted to consolidate his three lines into one, the Atlantic, Mississippi and Ohio, and planned to run this line to the

---

7.   *Ibid.*, pp. 115-116.
8.   *Ibid.*, p. 117.
9.   *Ibid.*, pp. 118-119.
10.   *Ibid.*, p. 122.

southwest Virginia coal fields, so he could haul the coal out through Hampton Roads.[11]

Another new political party entered the scene, the True Republican Party. The True Republicans opposed the Radicals and sought a moderate government. Gilbert C. Walker, a New York carpetbagger, was their candidate for governor, facing the Radical candidate H.H. Wells. The Conservatives initially nominated Withers, but at Mahone's insistence the Conservative Party threw its support behind Walker.[12]

Most Conservatives saw a new lease on life if Conservative candidates could win by smashing Radical rule and restoring political power to the "cavaliers"—the planter-capitalist class.[13]

Kemper, James Barbour, "Extra-Billy" Smith, and John Goode, Jr., opposed Walker. Kemper supported John Garrett, president of the Baltimore and Ohio Railroad, who was also affiliated with the Orange and Alexandria. His plan was to extend his line through Madison and the surrounding counties to southwest Virginia and haul the coal out through Alexandria.[14]

For the House of Delegates, Kemper supported William O. Fry. Mahone's candidate was James W. Walker, Jr.[15] Radical control was almost over in Virginia as the Conservatives flocked to the polls. In January 1870, Virginia's congressional delegation was allowed to take their seats and on January 26th, Virginia was readmitted to the Union. The election had been a bitterly contested one, and no doubt Mahone's money had been a determining factor in the outcome.

Gilbert C. Walker's administration proved to be the worst and the most corrupt in Virginia history. Such controversial issues as Ma-

---

11.   Moger, p. 10.
12.   *Ibid.*, p. 122; Moore, p. 14.
13.   Moore, p. 12.
14.   *Ibid.*, p. 10.
15.   Jones "Conservative Virginian," p. 122.

hone's railroad consolidation schemes and the state's sale of its railroad investments to fund the pre-war debt caused many Virginians to become disillusioned. By supporting Walker they had hoped to save the state from what they perceived to be Negro domination and ruin. Thousands felt their administration had sold them out to the railroads and bondholders; others simply resented a carpetbagger as governor. The people of Virginia were determined to see Virginia ruled by Virginians.[16]

---

16.   Moger, pp. 11-21.

Chapter 26

The Road to the Governor's Office

The Conservatives in the Virginia legislature sought to defend property rights and settle the state's debt as two of their main goals. The debt was at $45 million, the result of antebellum borrowing for the building of railroads and canals that were destroyed in the war. The improvements were lost, but the debt remained. The tax-paying ability of Virginians had been cut by two-thirds, and the state teetered on the verge of bankruptcy. Virginia wasn't alone in this economic predicament; all of the southern states suffered, primarily because of their investments in now-worthless bonds.[1]

The Conservatives were anxious to restore the state's good name by honoring the entire debt and as early as 1866 the General Assembly voted to do so. In 1871, however, Governor Walker presented a plan for Virginia to fund two-thirds of the debt, with West Virginia picking up the other third. A breakdown in negotiations between the states and legal difficulties foiled this plan. Walker's funding bill, which drastically over-estimated the state's resources and embroiled it in deficit spending, proved to be the most disastrous piece of economic legislation in the state's history.[2]

An attempt to get the bondholders to lower their interest rates

---

1.   Moore, p. 15.
2.   *Ibid.,* p. 16.

failed. The Conservatives tried to get the United States government to assume the state's war time debt, arguing that the state was now conquered territory. This , too, failed.[3]

The state split into two factions, the Funders and the Readjusters. The Funders, which included most Conservatives, believed that the people of the state should make the necessary financial sacrifices and shoulder the entire burden of debt to uphold the honor of the state. The Readjusters, on the other hand, wanted to adjust the debt downward to match the state's ability to pay. The Readjusters argued that northerners and foreigners owned the majority of the bonds and therefore had no legitimate claims on the state because they were responsible for contributing to the state's military defeat.[4]

There were several questions that played into the argument of the state debt. First, should interest have accrued during the war? Second, should the honor of the state be recognized as a primary factor in the economic world? Third, since Virginia suffered military occupation following the war, did the federal government considered the state a conquered territory, and if so, should the federal government assume the debt? Fourth, should the debt be reduced because of severe property damage suffered during the war, and, given the creation of the state of West Virginia, should the debt be reduced by one-third to compensate for the loss of that portion of taxable property? Fifth, since Virginia existed as Military District I from 1865-1870, who should be responsible for the debts incurred during that period? And finally, should debts owed creditors within Virginia be paid before those out of the state, particularly those in New York and London?[5] Kemper tended to be a Funder in most of these issues; however, no clear answers could be given to these

---

3.   *Ibid.*, p. 17.

4.   *Ibid.*, pp. 18-19.

5.   Dorothy M. Torpey *Hallowed Heritage: The Life of Virginia* (Richmond, 1961), p. 132.

complicated questions and solutions would be debated for years to come.

At this time Kemper held a number of important posts in both state and local levels of the Conservative Party. He readily gave aid to friends and party members in elections and helped secure positions for friends in the state government. He was called on often to advise legislators. He generally served as the political sage of Madison and vicinity.

He helped his old friend and wife's cousin, Henry G. Shackelford, to obtain a judgeship in Orange County and his friend, Wyatt Beazley of Greene County, to obtain the judgeship in Madison and Greene. He also worked to restore the office of adjutant-general to his old friend William Richardson, who was very anxious to reorganize the militia. Richardson was re-appointed to his former position by Governor Walker and soon new militia companies were formed, including some all Negro units.[6]

Kemper unsuccessfully sought the presidencies of the Chesapeake and Ohio and the Orange and Alexandria railroads, but was elected director of the Fredericksburg and Gordonsville Railroad. He continued to be a strong advocate of a rail connection for isolated Madison and Greene Counties and urged local businessmen to lend financial support to the plan. The Fredericksburg and Gordonsville declined to run a line west from Orange to Charlottesville through Madison and Greene, so Kemper tried to get the C & O to run a branch line from Staunton through Madison and Greene to Culpeper, which connected to Washington. He also contacted the Pennsylvania Central about running a line from Front Royal to Charlottesville. When his efforts to get a major railroad to come to this area failed,[7] he went to the Narrow Gauge Railway Company

6. Jones "Conservative Virginian," pp. 133-134.
7. Madison and Greene counties still do not have a railroad. At one time (in the 1920s and 1930s) Madison County did have a narrow gauge railroad operated by a timber company to get logs to market.

of New York and encouraged them to build a line from Culpeper to Stanardsville. Later plans led to discussion of an alternate route from Front Royal to Gordonsville by way of Chester Gap. Both Madison and Greene would have had to put up large sums of money (approximately $25,000 annually) to secure and maintain this line. This plan also failed.[8]

In June of 1870 the General Assembly passed the Southside Consolidation Act, which directly benefited Mahone's railroads, and then adjourned without passing any other legislation. Once again Mahone's money had gotten results, and Madison County was deprived of a railroad.[9]

Kemper was a senior member of the sixth district committee of the Conservative Party, and attended the convention held in Alexandria on September 29, 1870, where candidates were selected for the November congressional election. His wife died in October and he took no active part in the campaigning.

1871 began on a dismal note, with Kemper still grieving for Belle. The General Assembly of 1871 passed the "free Railroad law," and sold the state's stock in all lines except the Richmond, Fredericksburg and Potomac. Mahone fought the sale, but his enemies, the Bucktails, were too powerful. The Penn Central bought most of the lines, including the Richmond and Danville and the Richmond and Petersburg.[10]

Also passed by the General Assembly was Walker's Funding Act of 1871, which called for funding two-thirds of the state's debt by the sale of bonds bearing six per cent interest. The interest coupons from these bonds could be used to pay taxes and other obligations due the state.[11]

Kemper was urged by fellow Conservatives to take a leading

---

8. Jones "Conservative Virginian," pp. 136-138.
9. *Ibid.*, p. 138.
10. *Ibid.*, pp. 139-140.
11. *Ibid.*, p. 141.

Darrell T. Estes

Mountain Prospect the birthplace of James Lawson Kemper in a recent photo. Built about 1800 by his father, William Kemper, it is now the home of Judge and Mrs. Basil Burke, Jr.

This monument marks the Kemper family graveyard at Mountain Prospect. It honors Kemper's father (William Kemper, Nov. 6, 1776 to Oct. 29, 1853) and mother (Maria Kemper, Nov. 5, 1787 to Nov. 26, 1873) and names their children.
Darrell T. Estes

James Kemper in the spring of 1862, when he was colonel of the Seventh Virginia Infantry. The photo was taken by C.E. Jones & Vannerson in Richmond. *From the author's collection*

This photo was probably taken at the same time as the photo above. *From the author's collection*

Photograph of Kemper
following the war.
*Madison County Board
of Supervisors*

This photograph was
most likely taken after
Kemper's release from
prison, following his
wounding and capture at
Gettysburg.
*Manuscript print
collection, Special
Collections Dept.,
University of Virginia
Library*

The Kemper Mansion is on the main street in the town of Madison. Kemper and his family lived here from 1865 to 1882. The mansion is undergoing renovation.

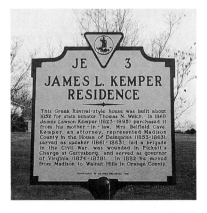

JE 3
JAMES L. KEMPER
RESIDENCE

This Greek Revival-style house was built about 1852 for state senator Thomas N. Welch. In 1868 James Lawson Kemper (1823-1895) purchased it from his mother-in-law, Mrs. Belfield Cave. Kemper, an attorney, represented Madison County in the House of Delegates (1853-1863), served as speaker (1861-1863), led a brigade in the Civil War, was wounded in Pickett's Charge at Gettysburg, and served as governor of Virginia (1874-1878). In 1882 he moved from Madison to Walnut Hills in Orange County.

After the war, Kemper used this tiny building behind the mansion to conduct his law practice.

The state historical marker, placed here by the Kemper-Fry-Strother Camp, Sons of Confederate Veterans, in 1992.

Mr. and Mrs. I.W. Jeannes
Kemper was the governor of Virginia when this photograph was taken, the culmination of many years of political service. He represented Madison County in the Virginia House of Delegates from 1853 to 1863, serving as Speaker of the House from 1861 to 1863. He served his state with distinction and great personal sacrifice during the war, and returned to the political arena to serve as her governor from 1874 to 1878.

This portrait of Kemper as a Confederate general hangs in the court room at Orange, Virginia. *Orange County Circuit Court*

Darrell T. Estes
Walnut Hills, Kemper's home in Orange County, as it looks today. It is now the home of Mr. and Mrs. I.W. Jeannes.

Nancy DeJarnette Berry
Painting of Walnut Hills as it appeared when Kemper lived there.

The James Lawson Kemper Memorial Bridge carries U.S. 15 across the Rapidan River between Madison and Orange counties. It was completed in September 1991.
Darrell T. Estes

James Lawson Kemper's grave in the small family cemetery at Walnut Hills. The gravesite is maintained by the Kemper-Fry-Strother Camp, Sons of Confederate Veterans.

The state historical marker on U.S. 15 at Madison Mills, Virginia, near the turnoff to Walnut Hills.
Darrell T. Estes

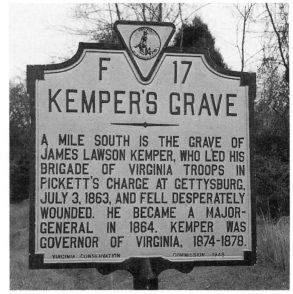

role in state politics. He did not, however, attend the convention of August 1871. Most Conservatives were dissatisfied with Walker and they started a "New Departure" movement to get control back in the hands of Virginians. Kemper, who represented what was good in Virginia politics—honesty, integrity, and dignity—figured largely in their plans.[12]

Kemper, meanwhile, helped to organize the Piedmont Agricultural Society in Madison, Orange and Culpeper counties. He was chosen a vice president from Madison and then unanimously elected president by the directors. He worked diligently selling stock subscriptions for the society. Similar societies were founded in Albemarle and Fauquier.[13]

In August he accompanied his son Meade to Washington to see him off to Boonville, Missouri, to attend his uncle Frederick's school.

By this time Kemper was ready, once again, to take an active role in politics. He was a consulting member of the Conservative's state executive committee for the seventh district and became the superintendent of Madison County.

The result of the election was a resounding Conservative victory, and Kemper had played in important role in it. Daniel A. Grimsley was re-elected to the Senate, and conservative candidates John R. Strother of Culpeper, Francis M. McMullen of Madison, W.R. Taliaferro of Orange, and George Bouton of Greene were all elected to the House of Delegates.[14]

After the election, Kemper was urged to take an even more active role in state politics. S. Bassett French assured him of strong support "from the mountains to the sea" for the gubernatorial election.[15] Kemper became more receptive to the encouragement of his

---

12. *Ibid.,* pp. 142-144.
13. *Ibid.,* pp. 144-145.
14. *Register of the General Assembly*
15. Kemper's papers U.Va.

friends and was urged by some to seek the seat in Congress from the seventh district. He attended the Conservative Party convention in June 1872, despite a carriage accident just prior to the meeting. He supported the presidential ticket of Horace Greeley and Benjamin Brown and was chosen presidential elector-at-large.[16]

Kemper, Sam Moore of Clarke County, James Barbour, and James G. Field of Orange were influential in the district convention to choose a candidate for congress. Kemper planned to support Barbour but couldn't go to the convention held in Alexandria. He expected the delegation from Madison to follow his advice, but the Madison delegates surprised everyone and supported Eppa Hunton. Kemper narrowly avoided a split with Barbour over the action of the Madison delegates.[17]

Kemper campaigned statewide for the Greeley-Brown ticket. In September alone he spoke in Wytheville, Salem, Lynchburg, Farmville, Danville, Halifax Court House, Madison Court House and Winchester. He was equally busy in the month of October.[18]

Kemper was as an eloquent, able and effective public speaker. Newspapers declared him to be an "eminent success" and reported that he left a "profound impression." As the campaign progressed, talk of Kemper for governor increased. Kemper had served in the halls of the legislature and on the field of battle. He represented the "true people of Virginia" and was recognized by the people of Virginia for his involvement in the "New Departure" that would eventually bring him to power.

Greeley and Brown lost the state by 1,975 votes. The ticket did, however, carry Madison County by 336 votes.[19]

Kemper was dissatisfied and disillusioned with the performance of Walker, and he began to look forward to the election of 1873.

---

16.   Jones "Conservative Virginian," pp. 150-152.
17.   *Ibid.,* p. 152.
18.   Richmond *Enquirer.*
19.   Jones "Conservative Virginian," p. 155.

Chapter 27

The Nomination for Governor

No figure in post-war Virginia politics combined so distinguished an ante-bellum political career with so fine and gallant a Confederate military record as James Lawson Kemper. His pre-war contributions were familiar to many, and his outstanding military service, especially his part in Pickett's Charge, was even more widely known. The physical evidence of his devotion and sacrifice to his native state was evident to all; his cane and pronounced limp were "clearly his greatest political asset."[1]

Although his post-war career up this this point was not devoted entirely to politics, he had played an active role, at critical times, in the effort to regain control of the state by Virginians. He had been active in the formation of the Conservative Party, had performed a yeoman service in the campaign of 1869, and had won considerable popularity in his vigorous state-wide campaign on behalf of Horace Greeley in 1872.

As early as August of 1872, Kemper was encouraged to seek the nomination for governor of Virginia. Some political analysts counted him as the strongest potential candidate in Northside Virginia, and in the winter of 1872-73, he was widely regarded as the

---

1.　　Jones "Conservative Virginian," p. 160; Moger, p. 21.

man most preferred for governor.

In March a trickle of letters of support and encouragement arrived at the post office in Madison. By June they were pouring in from all over the state.[2] Judge William Pope Dabney summed up Kemper's qualifications in his letter:

> Your long and prominent position in our legislature, your army record, your residence in a county which represents the sympathies of Eastern Virginia and the Valley, your late able canvas of the State as Conservative Elector . . . will undoubtedly insure you the nomination of the Conservative Convention. The fact that the State voted for Grant, will energize our party to bring every voter to the polls, which must insure our complete success.[3]

Although a favorite, Kemper was not the only one considered for governor. Among the dozen or so prominent men also mentioned as possible candidates, the strongest was Robert E. Withers, who had retired from the gubernatorial race in 1869 in favor of Walker. Withers, also an ex-Confederate, felt that the Conservative Party owed him the nomination because of his sacrifice in 1869.[4]

Withers, however, had acquired many enemies. The former Know-Nothing had been deeply involved in the railroad fight, and as an advocate of the Pennsylvania Central he had alienated the state's native railroad owners.

Kemper, on the other hand, had no active part in the bitter fight between Mahone and the northern railroads. He also possessed the full confidence of the old Democratic Party. He was accepted by

---

2.   *Ibid.*, pp. 158-159; Kemper papers U.Va.
3.   Kemper papers U.Va., Judge William Pope Dabney to Kemper January 14, 1873.
4.   *Ibid.*, p. 159.

the old line Whigs, and he was uncompromisingly anti-Walker.[5]

Mahone had become a vital influence in state politics. He had achieved the consolidation of his railroads and was now determined to keep the Bucktails from gaining further control over Virginia's railroads and diverting Virginia commerce to northern cities. Walker had been influenced by the Bucktails, and Mahone was determined to prevent Withers, whom he knew was sympathetic to the Bucktails, from getting the nomination to succeed him.[6]

Robert W. Hughes of Southwest Virginia, the Republican candidate, was sympathetic to Mahone's views, but Mahone didn't feel he could be elected. Mahone favored Judge Waller R. Staples of the Supreme Court of Appeals, a native of Montgomery County, but Judge Staples indicated in May that he would not seek the nomination for health reasons.[7]

Mahone then turned his attention to Kemper. On May 26, N.B. Meade, Joseph Mayo, and J.C. Shields, the publisher of the Richmond *Whig,* all Mahone men, interviewed Kemper on the railroad question. After being convinced that Kemper's views were in line with his own, Mahone wholeheartedly threw his support behind him.[8]

Mahone and his supporters were delighted with their new candidate. Mahone actively provided organization and direction to the efforts to garner support of the delegations across the state, except for Madison, Orange, Greene and Culpeper counties, which he left to Kemper's old friends. A lot of the work done in the Southside and the Southwest was done by Mahone himself, who took the pre-convention campaign very seriously. He traveled his lines daily, spending a considerable amount of time and handling a stag-

5.   Jones "Conservative Virginian," p. 161.
6.   *Ibid.,* p. 162; Moger, p. 22.
7.   *Ibid.,* p. 163; *Ibid.,* p. 22.
8.   *Ibid.,* p. 164; *Ibid.,* p. 23.

gering load of correspondence, often working from 8:00 AM until midnight.[9]

Kemper himself did not actively solicit the office. He was of the old school of Virginia statesmen who went by the time-honored maxim that an office such as that of the governor of Virginia was neither to be sought nor declined. Kemper let his supporters do the hand shaking and line up county delegates to the August convention. Many of the state's most influential men pledged their support. William Richardson and C.B. Porter were among those active in behind-the-scenes work.[10]

A large part of Mahone's contribution to Kemper's nomination was financing the pre-convention campaign. Mahone willingly backed Kemper with liberal contributions, paying active campaign workers $100 per month plus expenses and providing free passes over his railroads for campaign workers and delegates pledged to Kemper. He spent considerable sums in securing delegates in crucial areas and instructed his aides to spare no cost.[11]

Mahone met with his old railroad adversary, John S. Barbour, at Lynchburg in mid-June, and the two railroad presidents agreed to support Kemper in the interest of their lines.

Despite Kemper's open support of Virginia's railroads, he made it clear that he would not be controlled by any railroad ring or other special interest group. Kemper and Mahone had no open contact with one another, although on July 15 they did hold a secret meeting in Baltimore.[12]

Kemper was ill and unable to attend the Conservative Party convention held on August 6 and 7, one of the largest and most enthusiastic ever held. On the afternoon of the sixth, Kemper's friend, Michael G. Harman, was elected chairman. Another of Kemper's

---

9.   *Ibid.*, pp. 167-170.
10.   *Ibid.*, pp. 166 & 168.
11.   *Ibid.*, pp. 171-172.
12.   *Ibid.*, pp. 174-176.

friends, Thomas Bocock, was chosen as president. The nominations began with Charles S. Stringfellow, Mahone's paid attorney, delivering an elegant eulogy of Kemper, which received great applause. Dr. George E. Rives of Prince George County seconded the nomination. Supporting speeches were made by Dr. Samuel H. Moffitt of Rockingham, James Call of Rockingham, and Joseph Mayo of Richmond.[13]

On the first ballot, 39 counties voted solidly for Kemper, 19 voted for Withers, and 39 cast split votes. By 2:30 AM, Kemper's overwhelming strength was evident. Jubal Early and Lieutenant-Governor R.L. Montague made simultaneous motions and Kemper was nominated "with great enthusiasm made unanimous by acclimation." Mahone, with his broad-brimmed hundred-dollar Panama hat and cigar in mouth, with Stringfellow on one side and J. Hampden Chamberlayne on the other, remained in the background, but was obviously pleased when the vote was taken.[14]

As a show of sympathy, Withers was nominated for lieutenant-governor by James A. Walker, who wanted the position himself and had the support of Kemper and Mahone. It was understood that if nominated, Withers would not accept. When notified of his nomination, Withers returned to the convention to decline, but was met with such an ovation when entering the hall, that he accepted,[15] to the great disappointment of Mahone. Raleigh T. Daniel was nominated for attorney-general.[16]

Kemper, at home in Madison, was notified by telegraph of his nomination. Early the next day he telegraphed his acceptance from a railroad station in nearby Orange. His brief message was received

---

13.   *Ibid.*, pp. 180-181; Moger, p. 23; *Tyler's Quarterly Historical and Genealogical Magazine* vol. VI, no. 1, July 1924, p. 72.
14.   *Ibid.*, p. 184.
15.   Jack P. Maddex *The Virginian Conservatives 1867-1879: A Study in Reconstruction Politics* (Chapel Hill, North Carolina, 1970), p. 108.
16.   Jones, "Conservative Virginian," p. 185.

"with three cheers and a tiger." Kemper closed his acceptance with "a profound sense of its great responsibility, but without fear of defeat." The enthusiasm at the convention boiled over.[17]

Most Virginians considered the Conservative nomination the equivalent to an election. Kemper was assured he would be enrolled with the Lees, the Randolphs, the Henrys, the Gilmers, the Floyds, the Barbours, and the Letchers of Virginia.

W.F. Drinkard summed up the belief of many:

> You all don't know Kemper. He is the greatest man in the State.
> No railroad ring, or any other ring, can control him. I would
> vote for him against the world.[18]

---

17.   *Ibid.*, p. 184.
18.   *Ibid.*, pp. 185 & 157; Kemper papers U.Va.

Chapter 28

The Election of 1873

News of Kemper's nomination spread quickly to the far corners of the state. He had remained in the background during the nominating process and let others campaign for him, but as the standard bearer for his party, he was now obliged to take the stump. Political picnics and barbecues would enliven the race, but there would be a goodly amount of handshaking and speechmaking to be done. Hard work lay ahead of him.

Kemper's Radical opponent, Robert W. Hughes of Washington County, was a newspaper editor in Abingdon. He was recognized as a good writer, but was not a gifted speaker. Hughes came from an old Virginia family, had been a former states' rights Democrat, and after the war had turned to radicalism. To the Conservatives, he was looked upon as a turncoat—worse than a carpetbagger.[1]

The Republican ticket included C.P. Ramsdell, a carpetbagger from Surry County, for lieutenant governor and David Fultz, a unionist from Augusta County, for attorney general.

The Republicans and Conservatives both advocated liberal provision for public schools and affirmed the position of equality for both races. Both parties also called for completion of the James River and

---

1.   Jones "Conservative Virginian," p. 188.

Kanawha Canal.[2]

The Conservatives opposed a tax on tobacco and spirituous liquors, opposed radical rule in other southern states and pledged to judge Grant's administration fairly. They represented property owners, former Confederates, businessmen and professionals.[3]

The members of the Republican Party, a meld of Negroes, carpetbaggers, scalawags and unionists from the mountain regions, were perceived as radical, incompetent, propertyless and irresponsible. They were backed by the Radicals in congress.[4]

Soon after his nomination, Kemper received a flood of congratulatory letters from all across the state and from Georgia, Missouri, Texas and other southern states as well. Among them were letters of support from many former Confederates, including generals Williams C. Wickham, Jubal Early, Fitzhugh Lee, Eppa Hunton, "Extra-Billy" Smith and William H. Richardson, and former colonel John S. Mosby.[5]

All were particularly pleased that Kemper was a native Virginian and were sure he would lead the state well in the fight against the Radicals and the carpetbaggers. Kemper's supporters wanted to effect a crushing defeat in November that would forever wipe the Radicals from Virginia. To their advantage, the vast majority of the state's newspapers were owned by Conservatives. Their enthusiasm about Kemper's candidacy was echoed in newspapers in other southern states as well.[6]

Kemper's letter of acceptance to Thomas S. Bocock, president

2.   *Ibid.*, p. 189.
3.   *Ibid.*, p. 190.
4.   Moore, p. 14; "Henry A. Wise and the Campaign of 1873: Some Selected Letters from the papers of James Lawson Kemper" edited by James A. Bean, Jr. *Virginia Magazine of History and Biography* vol. 62, no. 3, July 1954, p. 321.
5.   Jones "Conservative Virginian," p. 190.
6.   *Ibid.*, p. 191.

of the state Conservative convention, ran in the Richmond newspapers on August 16th. It complimented the party on providing for a better government than that under Radical control. He called upon Virginia to "go forward with the work of restoring their beloved Commonwealth," and urged Virginians to ignore "resentment and passion" and move forward with a "spirit of conciliation." He assured the state that Conservative rule would mean "ascendancy of virtue and intelligence" in public service. He promised "equal protection and benefits" to all Virginians, promised to provide an economical and honest administration and he pledged "the greatest interests of education, immigration, and material development." He closed by saying "we will, under the blessing of God, inaugurate a new era of Virginia history."[7]

Kemper remained in Madison, anxious to begin campaigning at once.[8] Mahone and other Conservative Party leaders presented Kemper with the campaign plan on August 21st at the Exchange Hotel in Richmond. He was expected to campaign in southwestern Virginia almost the entire month of September, spend October in the Valley, and then hit the Northside and Tidewater, and finally concentrate on the Southside's large Negro population the last two weeks before the election. Arrangements were made for funding the campaign at this meeting which was attended by Kemper, R.E. Withers, R.T. Daniel, R.M.T. Hunter, J.E. Stewart, T.S. Bocock, Mahone, N.B. Meade and others.[9]

The grand kick-off rally was held in Richmond on the 22nd and was attended by a large, enthusiastic audience. Speeches were made by Governor Walker, Withers, Hunter, Joseph Mayo, Judge Robert Ould, Mayor A.M. Kelley, and Kemper. Three days later in Warrenton, Kemper and Withers faced Hughes and company for the first time, in a debate. Hughes spoke first, and his speech pri-

---

7. Richmond *Dispatch,* August 16, 1873.
8. Kemper papers U.Va.
9. Jones "Conservative Virginian," p. 194.

marily appealed to Negroes and the lower economic groups; he pledged himself a "friend of the poor man." Kemper accused Hughes of avoiding the issues, attacked his previous record, and belittled Hughes's argument that the Republicans were a relief party, saying, "True, they have relieved the southern people of nearly everything they ever had."[10]

During the campaign, Kemper spoke often of public education and of state finances, promising that he would put the state on a better footing and decrease the tax burden. He pointed out the effects of radical Republican rule in other southern states and assured Virginians that a Republican victory in Virginia would mean the same in the Old Dominion.[11] Kemper, the military hero, also attacked his opponent's war record. Hughes had held a safe job with the Richmond *Examiner* during the war.

From Warrenton, the campaign moved to Southwest Virginia, his opponent's home turf. On September 1st, Kemper spoke in Franklin County. On September 2nd, at Newburn in Pulaski County, he spoke for two hours before a large and enthusiastic crowd. On September 4th, at Hillsville in Carroll County, he was entertained by supporters after his speech. Men who fought in his command during the war provided a string band that drew a large crowd. In the following days, he spoke in Floyd, Scott and Tazewell counties.[12]

Campaign contributions were slow. Mahone contributed $1,000 in late August, and throughout the campaign he spent generously. Other important contributors were railroad magnate J.M. Robinson and N.T. McCready of Norfolk. Robinson, Mahone and W.C. Wickham provided free passes over their railroads for the candidate and his campaigners.[13]

---

10. Richmond *Dispatch*, August 26, 1873.
11. Jones "Conservative Virginian," pp. 197 & 199.
12. *Ibid.*, p. 203.
13. *Ibid.*, p. 205.

The Conservative organization proved to be effective. The committee sent out 30,000 documents, weekly circulars and scores of individual letters. As the campaign progressed, contributions increased and promises of support were received from all over the state.[14]

Between September 15th and 22nd, Kemper spoke in Tazewell, Smyth, Giles, Botetourt, Washington and Montgomery counties. In early October he spoke in Staunton, accompanied by former governor Letcher. He was in Harrisonburg on October 4th and in Luray on October 6th. He spoke before thousands in Winchester, gave a grand speech in Leesburg on the 13th, then moved on to Alexandria.[15]

Kemper proved to be the ideal campaigner. He was handsome, attractive in manner, courteous, chivalrous, alert, and of military bearing. He was known as an effective public speaker and attracted throngs of people wherever he went. The effects of his old wound were obvious to all who saw him and invoked sympathetic memories of the recent war and Kemper's near fatal sacrifices. Late in the campaign, he told a crowd at Farmville with great confidence, "You had better hear me, for you are now looking in the face of the next governor of Virginia."[16]

Kemper appealed strongly to the ex-Confederates. Former members of his command and other comrades filled the newspapers with letters and anecdotes and memories of their beloved general. Stories of his heroism greatly appealed to the old soldiers. One such story told of the battle of Seven Pines, where in his shirt sleeves, covered with mud, with his crescent shaped sword in hand, Kemper called out to his men, "Come on, my bloody heroes! Charge! Send these Devils to Hell!" His followers recounted his concerns for his poor worn-out soldiers and told stories of his

14.   *Ibid.*, p. 206.
15.   *Ibid.*, p. 207.
16.   Richmond *Dispatch,* October 25, 1873.

wounding and of the building of a rude pine coffin when it was thought he would die.[17]

Former members of his command formed the Kemper Kampaign Klub. They held rallies and fund raising activities, with meetings every night. Effective speakers took the stump for Kemper all across the state. His supporters worked day and night to get voters out on November 4th.[18]

Kemper continued his vigorous campaigning in Tidewater and Southside. On October 18th he was in Norfolk and three days later in Hampton. He visited the eastern shore at the urging of supporters in Accomack and Northampton counties. On October 23rd he attended a rally in Petersburg. His next stop was Farmville, where he told the crowd that he had traveled over 4,000 miles in 60 days and had made 60 speeches. He went on to Buckingham on the 26th, then Halifax Court House on the 27th. His last speech was in Charlottesville on November 3rd. He closed out his campaign on election day, in a letter "to the People of Virginia" in the Richmond *Whig*. He thanked the people for their support and urged them to go to the polls for a Conservative Party victory.[19]

One old friend Kemper kept in touch with during the campaign was Henry A. Wise; Kemper wrote to him often. Wise was an unreconstructed rebel and couldn't endorse the Conservative Party because of their cooperation with federal authorities. John Sargent Wise tried desperately to secure his father's public support for Kemper. The younger Wise finally wrote Kemper that his father "admire[s] your Spirit and gallantry [as a] . . . life long and ardent friend and gallant Confederate leader."[20] That was as far as Wise would go in endorsing Kemper, although he probably did vote for

---

17.   Nelson M. Blake *William Mahone of Virginia Soldier and Political Insurgent* (Richmond, Virginia, 1935), p. 140.
18.   Jones "Conservative Virginian," pp. 209-211.
19.   *Ibid.*, pp. 211-212.
20.   *Virginia Magazine of History and Biography* July 1954, p. 324.

him.

The spirited, bitterly fought contest and a sunny, warm fall day combined to bring a record number of voters to the polls. Kemper carried 68 counties and the cities of Richmond, Norfolk, Fredericksburg, Alexandria, Staunton and Winchester. Hughes carried 31 counties and four cities. Out of 213,519 votes cast, Kemper got 121,812, to win by over 30,000 votes, the largest margin ever in a Virginia gubernatorial election.[21]

Radicals outside the state feared the Conservative victory as a sign of a change in power. The Democrats throughout the nation, on the other hand, drew encouragement it.[22] The election of 1873 amounted to a death blow to radicalism in Virginia.

Kemper received scores of congratulatory letters from all over Virginia and across the nation. One correspondent called his success "the most important victory . . . ever won in our country."[23] Another wrote, "Let me congratulate you on the glorious triumph of the Conservative Party in the State, not merely because you are its head, but because its success is due in so large a degree to your energy and talent."[24] Yet another wrote, "Permit me to congratulate you and also the people of Virginia upon your triumphant election. I feel that in Virginia we are safe from radical rule, not only for the next four years, but for all time to come."[25]

Kemper's victory was truly a triumph; he was the hero of the state. Celebrations were held all over the state by canvassers, campaign officers, and military organizations. The Kemper Kampaign Klub held an elaborate party in Richmond on the occasion of Kem-

---

21. *Ibid.*, p. 342.
22. Jones "Conservative Virginian," pp. 215-216.
23. Kemper papers U.Va., Thomas P. Atkinson of Amelia County to Kemper.
24. *Ibid.*, William J. Robertson to Kemper November 19, 1873.
25. *Ibid.*, Mann Spitler to Kemper, November 7, 1873.

per's first visit following the election.[26]

Privately he was overjoyed with the result of the long, hot, hard-fought campaign, but he shunned all public celebrations in his honor. He proudly proclaimed himself as "not of a class or a party, but of the whole people."

---

26.   Jones "Conservative Virginian," p. 217.

Chapter 29

The First Year of Kemper's Administration

At age 50, the newly-elected governor of Virginia was a strikingly handsome man with a formidable black beard who looked and acted much older than his years, an unhappy man who terribly missed his late wife and who drank heavily to ease the constant pain of his war wounds. His six children were the only joy in his life. "You ought just to see me," he wrote to a friend. "Although in pain, my children have made me younger and my bosom is full of roses."[1]

Before moving to Richmond, Kemper arranged with James G. Field of Culpeper and Judge E.R. Watson of Charlottesville to handle legal cases that he could not complete before January. His brother-in-law, Benjamin Cave, was to look after his agricultural interests and personal affairs in Madison.[2]

Kemper's old friend, William Richardson, was in Richmond making ready the governor's mansion. Richardson hired a female servant and a cook and engaged the services of Oliver, the private servant of Governor Walker, as the butler. Miss Augusta Daniel, the daughter of the new attorney general, was engaged as gov-

---

1. William Seale *Virginia's Executive Mansion* (Richmond, Virginia, 1988).
2. Jones "Conservative Virginian," p. 218.

erness for the children. The matter of finding a suitable receptionist was more difficult. Since Kemper was a widower, he was considered fair game, and quite a competition ensued. Kemper sought to avoid wagging tongues by insisting that the lady of the mansion be an "ancient female." At least one candidate was turned down because she had not attained the age of 50-60. No suitable lady presented herself, and Kemper's mother-in-law or Mrs. Henry Heth served as official hostess.[3]

The outgoing governor had earned a reputation for extravagance at the state's expense. Kemper wished to make a sharp departure from what he considered "much needless expense about the executive department." He sought "simplicity to characterize his administration" and wanted none of Walker's "foolery."[4] He refused to appoint an aide on the grounds that a paid staff was a "New York innovation;" his entire personal staff consisted only of his son Meade.[5] Just before the inauguration, Kemper declined a gift of "a splendid equipage and horses offered by his admirers."[6]

Kemper traveled to Richmond on December 2nd in excellent spirits and health and conferred with Walker, who decided that he would not send a concluding message to the General Assembly.[7] After several days in Richmond, Kemper returned to Madison Court House, where he dealt with letters of congratulation and advice and applications for positions in the new administration.[8]

The most controversial issue facing the Conservative Party, one that needed to be addressed almost immediately, was the state's relationship with the Grant administration. One faction of the party

3.   *Ibid.*, p. 219; Seale; Kemper papers U.Va.
4.   Kemper papers U.Va.
5.   Kemper papers U.Va.; Jones "Conservative Virginian," p. 220; Seale.
6.   Staunton *Spectator,* December 30, 1873.
7.   Kemper papers U.Va.
8.   Jones "Conservative Virginian," p. 220.

represented the unreconstructed rebels led by Jubal Early. The other faction of former Confederate officers urged general support of Grant and was led by John S. Mosby. John Scott of Warrenton, another supporter of Grant's, met with the president in late November and shortly afterwards had a private meeting with Kemper, at which he presented an invitation for Kemper to visit the president following the inauguration. Scott and Mosby wanted Kemper to work closely with the president. Kemper didn't want to appear closely associated with Grant, but did want to be in a position to throw his weight against the civil rights bill being debated in Congress.[9]

In preparing his inaugural address, Kemper was careful not to appear hostile toward Grant, pledging impartiality and promising cooperation. He conferred with James Barbour concerning the message in Gordonsville in late December, and met with Mosby on the 31st in Richmond. After their meeting, Mosby went to Washington to complete arrangements for Kemper to visit with Grant.[10]

Despite the urging of Governor Walker, the Kemper Kampaign Klub and others, Kemper refused a formal and imposing ceremony. He scheduled a quiet, unostentatious inaugural in the "cherished custom and tradition of the commonwealth."[11] The simple ceremony began at 3:00 PM on January 1, 1874. The Richmond *Dispatch* reported that Kemper was sworn in almost before he knew it. Only Governor Walker, Kemper, his son Meade and a few friends were present in the western reception room of the executive mansion. Judge E.H. Fitzhugh administered the oath of office.[12]

Shortly after the brief, almost private, ceremony, Kemper sent his written message to the General Assembly. The relatively short message discussed the major issues of the day: the relationship be-

9. *Ibid.*, pp. 221-222.
10. *Ibid.*, p. 222.
11. *Ibid.*, p. 223.
12. Richmond *Dispatch,* January 2, 1874.

tween the races, immigration, relations with other states, education and the debt. He reiterated his feelings on paying the debt, saying, "Obligations to public creditors binding the honor and good faith of the Commonwealth should be fulfilled to the utmost of our ability in any event and under all circumstances." He demanded Virginia's right to self-government and called for the abolishment of all unnecessary state offices.[13] His message was met with general approval of the majority of the people of Virginia and was met with warm approval in the press and in Congress.

Kemper encountered several obstacles early in his administration. Walker had filled public offices with anti-Kemper men, extreme conservatives or "Bourbons" who were set against his administration, as were the carpetbaggers deeply entrenched in the state government. Kemper saw dozens of people daily, worked closely with the General Assembly and handled a voluminous correspondence.

In late January the Virginia papers reported Kemper's invitation to visit President Grant and discuss southern affairs. Most Conservatives endorsed Kemper's decision to see the president. Grant was dissatisfied with the radical wing of the Republican Party and sought support among the conservative statesmen in the South. Kemper was mainly concerned with the defeat of the civil rights bill. The meeting which took place at the White House on February 12, was reportedly warm and hospitable, but the details were never made public.[14]

In early March, Kemper was faced with the first great crisis of his administration. On March 1, the House of Delegates passed Senate Bill Number 5, which transferred the city government of Petersburg from elected officials to a board of commissioners appointed by the city judge. The black majority of the city had

13. *House Journal,* January 1, 1874.
14. Jones "Conservative Virginian," p. 227.

elected a Republican-dominated city council, and it was at the insistence of the white population of the city that the General Assembly took the drastic step of changing the city's charter to put control of the municipal government into the hands of a judge appointed by the General Assembly. This would prove to be the most emotion-packed and most significant event of Kemper's entire term.[15]

Kemper gave days of thought to the bill and sought the advice of his friends. The popular solution encouraged by his mostly-white constituency would be for him to give his approval, but he could not deny the ultimate fact that this bill denied the right of self-government to the citizens of Petersburg.[16]

On March 12th, Kemper vetoed the bill. His four-page veto message to the General Assembly charged that the bill was unconstitutional and inexpedient, that it infringed on the Bill of Rights and was a blatant violation of the political rights of the city's citizens. He asserted that the bill subverted "[the] great cornerstone . . . principle . . . of republican liberty . . . that all government derives its just power from consent of the governed." He went on to state that the implementation of the bill would "sow seed of fresh irritation and strife between races," that it would "discourage immigration and capitol" from abroad and "sound a provocation to federal interference in our domestic affairs." [17]

Reaction to Kemper's veto was immediate. The governor was burned in effigy in Richmond and Petersburg. He was denounced by the Petersburg press. He was accused of having deserted the "white man's party" and having "sold the state to Grant." He received several anonymous threatening letters. The return of the bill to the Senate touched off a big fight against the governor led by senators George Hundley of Fluvanna and Samuel Moffitt. Sena-

---

15. *Ibid.*, p. 228; Moger, p. 25.
16. *Ibid.*, p. 228.
17. *Senate Journal* 1874, pp. 283-287.

tors Alexander B. Cochran of Augusta and Henry W. Thomas of Fairfax led the able defense of Kemper's action. The veto was sustained in the Senate by a vote of 25 to 13.[18]

An overwhelmingly favorable reaction was as swift in coming about as was the initial harsh criticism. Kemper's stand produced the greatest and most enthusiastic endorsements, congratulations and vows of support ever given a Virginia governor. Newspapers across the nation praised Kemper's "brave act" and "high statesmanship."[19] Alexander H. Stephens called Kemper's veto "[an] exceedingly able document" written by a "great and good man."[20]

The vote demonstrated to the federal government and the North that Virginia recognized the rights of blacks and would defend these rights. The vote also won Kemper wide-spread national acclaim and mention of a possible vice-presidential nomination of the Democratic Party in 1876.

The excitement over Kemper's veto died down some in late March, when the Conservative candidates won a majority of the offices in the Petersburg city elections. Then the federal district attorney accused the city of "irregularities" and thirty federal troops were sent to the city to keep the peace. Kemper boldly denounced the "despotic invasion" and called for removal of the troops, which he claimed were sent to intimidate the people for purely "partisan purposes." The troops were soon removed and the issue died down for the time being.[21]

Kemper then turned his attention to other matters. He sought early on to provide the state with an honest administration. He was determined from the start to fight corruption in state government. As early as January, Kemper had suspended the secretary of the

18.   Jones "Conservative Virginian," pp. 230-231; Moger, p. 26.
19.   *Ibid.*, p. 231.
20.   Kemper papers U.Va., Alexander H. Stephens to Kemper, March 18, 1874.
21.   Jones "Conservative Virginian," pp. 231-234; Moger, p. 26.

board of the sinking fund, W.D. Coleman, for misconduct and initiated an investigation by the General Assembly of discrepancies in the fund. In March the state treasurer, Joseph Mayo, was charged with embezzlement and removed from office. Kemper also fired several penitentiary officials for swindling the government on purchases. Former governor Walker was implicated in many of the wrongdoings. Following a thorough investigation of the entire state government, Kemper forbade "gaming and drunkenness" among officials, especially those in the executive department. Kemper's passion for good honest government was also evident by appointments he made to public office.[22]

On March 27th, he sent a message to the legislature on state finances. On April 23rd, he sent another message regarding proposed amendments to the Underwood constitution; Kemper recommended that a whole new constitution be framed.[23]

On May 28th, the Federal government once again interfered in the operation of the city government of Petersburg. U.S. Attorney General George W. Williams, at the request of Republican representative James H. Platt of Norfolk, directed the marshal of the eastern district of Virginia to resist alleged disorders in Petersburg, promising military support if warranted. This action was taken while President Grant was away from Washington, and he knew nothing of what was going on. Kemper sent a stinging letter to the president, protesting the federal action in Virginia and affirming Virginia's right to self-government. He demanded the president redress the "wrongs" committed and prevent their reoccurrence.[24]

Kemper was again praised all across the nation for his stance. Mosby and others expressed their favor of a Grant-Kemper ticket in the next election. This caused quite a stir in the state's newspapers, forcing Kemper to send John Scott a letter refusing to have

22.   *Ibid.*, pp. 241-246; Moore, p. 24.
23.   *Ibid.*, pp. 234-235.
24.   *Ibid.*, p. 236.

his name mentioned as a possible candidate on a ticket with Grant and opposing a third term for Grant.[25]

Besides matters of policy and law, there were also matters of a practical nature to be dealt with. The General Assembly had directed Kemper to have new state seals made that spring, the old seals having either been stolen or mislaid during the war. Following the war, former governor Francis Pierpoint had made an unauthorized, unsatisfactory seal with the incorrect motto "Liberty & Union." Kemper had the new seals prepared according to the General Assembly's specifications for size and use.[26]

After an active spring, Kemper took some time off for fishing in the late summer. He and state treasurer R.M.T. Hunter (who had replaced the ousted Joseph Mayo), along with Secretary of State James McDonald and other dignitaries took a week's expedition on the Potomac.[27] During his tenure, Kemper took annual summer holidays of seven to ten days and enjoyed periodic quiet weekends at home in Madison.[28]

Kemper led a relatively simple life as governor. Social affairs at the executive mansion were held in a simple country style. He did entertain frequently with dinners, breakfasts, and occasional receptions. Now and then, he hosted a dance, but he did not allow his daughters to waltz. Beaux were advised to be gone by 10:00 PM or Oliver would present them with their hat and coat on the dance floor. The governor opened the mansion each New Year's day to receive guests and well wishers.[29]

Kemper's devotion to the Jeffersonian idea of frugal and simple government was evident in his first year in office. He took a mod-

25.   *Ibid.*, p. 237.
26.   *William and Mary College Quarterly Historical Magazine*, no. 1, vol. III, July 1894.
27.   Jones "Conservative Virginian," p. 240.
28.   *Ibid.*, p. 356.
29.   *Ibid.*, p. 356.

erate course in dealing with problems he faced. He won a wide-spread reputation for his defense of civil rights for blacks. Kemper was justifiably proud of his part in improving race relations in the state; white Virginians came to accept, under Kemper's leadership, black suffrage, education, and office holding. Some blacks even began to participate in conservative politics.

Chapter 30

Kemper and the Public Debt

The public debt was to be the most important matter dealt with during the Kemper administration, and it was certainly the greatest problem facing the state that first year. Kemper felt that the federal government should assume Virginia's war-time debt as a consequence of conquered territory. He was not optimistic about this happening, however. He warned Virginians not to depend solely or mainly upon assistance and relief from the central government,[1] but instead sought not only to obtain help from others, but also looked for ways that Virginians might help themselves. He felt that above all else, to protect the honor and good faith of the commonwealth, the debts should be fulfilled to the best of the state's ability to pay.

Kemper emphasized strict accountability, the taxing of legitimate subjects and creation of a permanent fiscal policy. He called for automatic payment of interest to the state's creditors.[2]

The governor felt that the restoration of the public credit was absolutely necessary for influx of immigration and capital.[3] He emphasized that punctual payment of utmost interest would restore

1.   *House Journal* "Inaugural Message" January 1, 1874.
2.   *Ibid.*
3.   *Ibid.*

confidence, good understanding and respect. To achieve this, he said, Virginia needed a just and efficient system of taxation. He argued against an increase in the lands tax, but new taxes were needed to make up for losses in taxable property, worth $748 million in 1860 and just $337 million in 1873. He needed time to come up with a workable solution.[4]

Although Kemper was generally perceived as a Funder, he did believe there were limits beyond which the state could not be expected to pay. He found that the state was not prepared to meet the obligations of the Funding Act and felt the debt should be modified somewhat.[5]

Kemper asserted that the Funding Act was a disastrous mistake passed by inexperienced legislators and based upon exaggerated estimates made by the ex-governor. He charged that the stock gamblers and money changers were involved in its passage, which led to corruption and speculation. Actually the Funding Act was unsatisfactory to both parties; it burdened the state with high taxes, and creditors found securities heavily depreciated and interest long overdue.[6]

He felt the bondholders would accept an adjustment if regular and punctual payment of two-thirds of the accruing interest was made. He wanted to treat all debts the same, with no preferred treatment to any, and wanted a permanent law to specify and set aside taxes to pay the debt.[7]

On March 27th Kemper recommended that the legislature appoint two commissioners to meet with representatives of the creditors to negotiate a solution. His message to both legislators and creditors stressed the need for cooperation. Most of the bondholders in New York were impressed, but the bondholders in London

---

4. *Ibid.*
5. Jones "Conservative Virginian," pp. 248-249.
6. *House Journal* "Financial Message" March 27, 1874.
7. *Ibid.*

were especially vocal in their disapproval. Most were thankful that Kemper had attacked the problem so promptly and early in the administration, though, and this message further enhanced his reputation.[8]

The General Assembly acted swiftly. Both houses considered Kemper's proposal and on April 10th the House of Delegates passed a resolution supporting the governor's plan. On April 14th the Senate did likewise and requested the governor call the conference. The legislature appointed Kemper and state treasurer R.M.T. Hunter to represent the state.[9]

At the same time, the General Assembly also passed a bill calling for payment of four per cent interest on six per cent bonds and three and one-third per cent on five per cent bonds. Part of the proposal called for a new comprehensive tax law that promised greater yields, which would give Kemper the edge he needed in dealing with the creditors. This action confirmed that Virginia was doing everything possible to meet her obligations.

The conference was held in Richmond on November 10. Judge H.W. Thomas of Alexandria was the chairman and James H. Dooley of Richmond was the secretary. Many of the bondholders were present, represented by their agents or by Richmond lawyers. Some members of the General Assembly and the executive department were in attendance.[10]

Kemper opened the conference by stating that the interests of the debtor and creditor were the same and reviewing the history of the Funding Act. He painted a gloomy picture of the state's economy, vividly described the poverty and heavy financial burdens faced by the people of Virginia. He asserted that the state was raising all revenue possible and paying its creditors all it could. He

---

8.   Jones "Conservative Virginian," p. 257.
9.   *Ibid.*, p. 259.
10. *Ibid.*, p. 262.

called for adjustment.[11]

Some of the bondholders were impressed with Kemper's report, but others (the British) were very critical. Eventually, after much discussion, Kemper's plan was adopted and Kemper was warmly congratulated for his success. It appeared that Virginia was once again on a firm financial footing.[12]

On December 2, 1874, Kemper sent his second annual message to the General Assembly. He was highly pleased at the outcome of the bondholders' conference and his address carried the tone of optimism. He praised the legislators for taking the first step in solving the problem. He took understandable pride in his administrative reforms and his curtailments of unnecessary expenditures. He mentioned the perils of the depressed population, especially farmers and laborers. He also called for a tax on wines and liquors.[13] He was ready to begin his second year as governor.

11. *Ibid.*, p. 263.
12. *Ibid.*, pp. 265-266.
13. *Ibid.*, pp. 276-278.

Chapter 31

The Second and Third Years

Kemper's second annual message to the General Assembly dealt with a wider variety of issues than had been addressed previously. Besides the debt, Kemper identified problems in the criminal justice system, calling for more fines as a less costly alternative to imprisonment and advocating a complete overhaul of the penitentiary system. He called attention to the boundary dispute between Maryland and Virginia, the pardoning powers of the governor, and called for the establishment of a state bureau of statistics. He encouraged immigration, the fishing industry, sheep raising and the completion of the James River and Kanawha Canal. His address also touched on the regulation of railroads, inspection of tobacco and relations with the federal government.[1]

On January 12, 1875, Kemper condemned the conduct of federal troops still stationed in Louisiana. The troops refused to allow legislators to take their seats and held courts martial of private citizens. Kemper detested the presence of military law and the abuse of civil liberties. Several days later, following the governor's condemnation, the General Assembly passed a resolution likewise condemning what was going on in that sister southern state.[2]

---

1.   *House Journal* "Annual Message" December 2, 1874.
2.   Jones "Conservative Virginian," p. 284.

Immigration, both from other states and from foreign nations was of major significance at this time. Immigrants provided a sorely needed market for surplus lands, created a new source of taxation and provided industry with highly skilled labor. Kemper created a Board of Immigration to facilitate immigration and encourage the immigrants to stay in Virginia once they got here.[3]

A highlight of the second year was the erection and dedication of sculptor J.H. Foley's impressive statue of Stonewall Jackson. The legislature appropriated $10,000 and a board of commissioners consisting of Kemper, Jubal Early, and two members of the General Assembly, John L. Eubank and William B. Taliaferro, was appointed. Former Confederate general Joseph E. Johnston was chosen as marshal-in-chief for the October 26th dedication. Another former Confederate, Henry Heth, was in charge of organizing the parade. President Jefferson Davis was invited but could not attend. Mrs. Jackson and her daughter Julia were to attend and were invited to stay at the executive mansion.[4]

A controversy arose over a Negro militia company's request to participate in the parade. Early, who was living in Lynchburg, wrote that to allow them to participate was a "disgrace and indignity to the memory of Jackson, and an insult to all Confederates who have any respect for themselves left." Kemper disagreed, feeling it would be unjust and wrong to reject them. Other former Confederates sided with Kemper, notably Fitzhugh Lee. Kemper finally decided to allow the Negroes to participate, and Heth assigned them a position in the parade.[5]

Early dashed off an insulting letter to Kemper denouncing the plans and the admission of the Negroes. Kemper defended his action and concluded his response by saying "the programme is fixed: all Hell can't change it." He begged Early not to come to

3. *Ibid.*, p. 297.
4. *Ibid.*, p. 299.
5. *Ibid.*, p. 300; Moger, p. 26.

Richmond and warned "if trouble comes . . . you will be responsible for it." Early continued to denounce Kemper and came to Richmond anyway.[6]

The capital city was gaily decorated for the event with Confederate flags, wreaths, posters, pictures, etc. A hundred thousand people from all over the South were in attendance. The procession stepped off at 12:30 PM, led by Joseph Johnston and the First Virginia regiment, followed by numerous military commands. Then came Governor Kemper in his carriage with Mrs. Jackson, followed by state and federal officials, distinguished Confederates, survivors of Jackson's staff, and regiments and civic clubs. For some unknown reason, the Negro volunteers did not march in the parade after all.[7]

The procession was two to three miles long and took one hour to file into Court Square. The Richmond *Enquirer* reported that "not less than 100,000 people crowded in."[8] Those on the speaker's stand were a virtual who's who of Confederate leaders and Virginia statesmen. In a long and flowery speech, Kemper said the monument was a tribute to Jackson's virtue and genius and would be cherished by every American with national pride as one of the noblest memorials of a common heritage of glory. He introduced the featured orator, Dr. Moses D. Hogue of St. Paul's Episcopal Church in Richmond, who spoke on the life and character of Jackson. Following the speeches, the statue, poised on a massive pedestal of Virginia granite on the green behind the capitol, was unveiled with bands playing, choirs singing, and infantry and artillery saluting.[9] That night there was a brilliant fireworks display followed by a reception for Mrs. Jackson at the executive mansion.

There were frequent occasions to honor Confederate heroes in

---

6. *Ibid.*, p. 302.
7. *Ibid.*, p. 302; Moger, p. 26.
8. Richmond *Enquirer*, October 27, 1875.
9. Jones "Conservative Virginian," p. 303.

Richmond. Just two days prior to the Jackson ceremony, Kemper participated when his old commander, General Pickett was laid to rest at Hollywood Cemetery. The Negro militia companies marched in Pickett's imposing procession, lending more confusion as to why they did not march in Jackson's procession.[10]

All of Kemper's family came to Richmond to spend Christmas with him that year, filling his heart with joy.[11]

The year 1876, Kemper's third in office, would see both a presidential election and the celebration of the nation's centennial. Still wrestling with the repayment of the debt, Kemper advocated reducing the size of the legislature as a cost savings measure. After much discussion, the House of Delegates was reduced from 132 to 100 members and a decision to meet bi-annually instead of annually further reduced costs.[12]

Kemper's proposed stamp tax of thirty cents per gallon on spirituous liquors was a continuing issue. He addressed such diverse issues as immigration, the oyster industry, the criminal justice system, tobacco inspections, the James River and Kanawha Canal, the Maryland boundary arbitration, government reform, the creation of a bureau of statistics, the fishing industry, the University of Virginia and revision of the state's carpetbagger constitution.

Kemper renewed his commitment to clean, honest government. It was evident that this sentimentalist would go to extreme measures to protect the pristine integrity of the Commonwealth. He advocated a return to the old system of voice voting over the secret ballot then in use. He sincerely felt that a person should feel strongly enough about a candidate that he shouldn't mind voting for him in public.[13]

Thirty-four years after his address at Washington College in

10.   *Ibid.*, p. 303.
11.   *Ibid.*, pp. 304-305.
12.   Bean, p. 146.
13.   Jones "Conservative Virginian," p. 310.

1842, Kemper was still an advocate of state supported public schools. He called on the state's educators to advise the legislature of their specific problems, and he urged all Virginians to endorse his policy of free schools. The state's school budget for 1875-76 was $443,000, a record allocation. The Conservative Party endorsed Kemper's policy and gave strong support to the state's school system. More children were to attend school during Kemper's term than ever before.[14]

In July the governor was terribly embarrassed by his son and private secretary, Meade, who went on a drunken spree in New York and Philadelphia, caused quite a ruckus, and spent $500 of his father's personal funds. The newspapers had a field day with the news, and Kemper had to make a public apology for his son's irresponsible behavior.[15]

A national centennial celebration was to be held in Philadephia in October 1876. John D. Imboden was to head the state's centennial board, and plans were made to exhibit Virginia's resources. Many legislators were not sure whether Virginia should participate in the event since the South was still being discriminated against and treated as conquered territory. They felt that to boycott the event would show the South's opposition to the Reconstruction Act. Kemper, on the other hand, felt that Virginia should go to Philadelphia in the spirit of reconciliation.[16]

The legislature eventually declined to appropriate funds for the project, so Virginia had no official display at the celebration. As part of the festivities, Kemper and the governors of the other thirteen original colonies were asked to host receptions in honor of the centennial. Virginia's reception was to be held on October 19th, the anniversary of the battle of Yorktown in the Revolutionary War.

14. *Ibid.*, pp. 319-322.
15. *Ibid.*, p. 333.
16. *Ibid.*, pp. 311-312; *Senate Journal* 1875-76, "Governor's Annual Message" December 1, 1875.

Kemper was not enthusiastic about going along with what most Virginians felt was a big Yankee show but felt that if other states were going to participate, then so should Virginia. On October 7th, after much thought on the matter, Kemper declined the offer to host the Virginia Day reception in Philadelphia, citing health reasons and the fact that the legislature did not support Virginia's participation. The people of Virginia overwhelmingly approved, but the governor's action got mixed response elsewhere in the nation.[17]

The national elections loomed large that year. Kemper hoped that former Union general Winfield Scott Hancock would get the Democratic nomination for president at the national convention in St. Louis. He was sorely disappointed when Samuel J. Tilden of Brooklyn, New York, was nominated to oppose Rutherford B. Hayes, and he chose not to take an active role in the campaign.[18]

The campaign was bitter, rough and hard fought in Virginia. There was a fear of a black uprising, and the governor received calls for arms from militia units and citizens committees. The racial tension appeared to be the worst in Mecklenburg, Prince Edward, Albemarle, Madison and Appomattox counties and the city of Lynchburg. Kemper opposed sending arms, fearing a race war. He instead sought a peaceful solution to the problem.

Things got so bad that federal troops again intervened in Petersburg. The governor was appalled at this federal interference and protested this intimidating action as a "despotic invasion."

Hayes was elected president, although Virginia and most other Southern states went for Tilden. After the election, the race situation cooled down.[19]

---

17.   *Ibid.,* pp. 330-333.
18.   *Ibid.,* p. 326.
19.   *Ibid.,* pp. 326-329.

Chapter 32

Final Year as Governor

K emper began 1877, the last year of his term as governor, on an optimistic note. His message to the legislature again dealt primarily with the debt and public finances; he reiterated the paramount obligation of re-establishing the state's credit and reported $200,000 more in revenue in the previous year than the past six years, with expenses of $108,986 less.[1]

Other issues that year included the school fund, the penitentiary system, lunatic asylums, tobacco inspection, and the bureau of statistics. He settled the boundary dispute with Maryland by which Virginia acquired valuable oyster beds. He called for doing away with public capital punishment and decried the recent federal intervention in Petersburg.[2]

He admonished the General Assembly that internal improvements required a great deal of attention. For example, the C & O Railroad had gone into receivership in 1875, with the state holding $5 million worth of stock. In December 1876 the attorney general indicated that a sale was probable. Kemper sent a special message to the legislature calling for the courts to delay further action until

---

1.   Jones "Conservative Virginian," pp. 336-337.
2.   *House Journal* 1876-77 "Governor's Annual Message" December 6, 1876.

the state could investigate the matter. The legislature failed to take action, and the railroad was sold on April 2, 1878, for only $2,750,000.[3]

Another matter of particular interest to Kemper was the completion of the James River and Kanawha Canal. The state held stock in the company worth $10,400,000. Kemper saw its completion as essential in conveying coal and iron ore to markets.[4]

On July 3rd, Kemper spoke at the first awarding of the Jackson-Hope medals to cadets L.H. Strother and E.M. Davidson of the Virginia Military Institute. The medals were sponsored by British admirers of Stonewall Jackson led by the Honorable Beresford Hope, and were to be awarded to the first and second most academically distinguished cadets at the institute.[5]

That fall, President Hayes paid an official visit to Virginia. The president, the governor and a distinguished party of state and national dignitaries watched the running of the Hermitage Cup on October 31st, during the state fair. President Hayes was warmly received by the large crowd. A simple reception was held at the governor's mansion following the race. In respect for Mrs. Hayes's temperance policy, the only beverage served was ice water.[6]

The Conservative Party chose F.W.M. Holliday as its candidate for governor from a large field of possibles that included William Mahone, William B. Taliaferro and Fitzhugh Lee. James A. Walker and James G. Field rounded out the ticket. As it turned out, the Conservative candidates were unopposed in the November election, and Holliday breezed into office.[7]

The governor's health began to deteriorate drastically, although

3.   Jones "Conservative Virginian," p. 347.
4.   *Ibid.,* p. 349.
5.   Lester Jesse Cappon *Bibliography of Virginia History Since 1865* (Charlottesville, Virginia, 1930), p. 3747.
6.   Jones "Conservative Virginian," p. 354; Seale.
7.   *Ibid.,* p. 352.

he admitted he had been partially paralyzed for years. He fell ill often—most seriously in November of 1877.[8] He was ready to return to Madison.

In his short tenure as governor, Kemper restored honesty and integrity to state government in Virginia. He closed his farewell message to the legislature with the following words:

> If my official service has been worthy of Virginia, then it shall speak for itself. If in aught I have been unfaithful or unequal to the high trust which a generous people committed to my charge, then no words of ingenious defense or apology can change faults into virtues. All I know and all I dare affirm is that having stood steadfastly against every opposer for what I have adjudged to be truth and the right, I shall now deliver into the hands of my successor the crown of Virginia's honor, without a stain or spot or blemish sullying its purity or its traditional glory.[9]

---

8. Jones "Conservative Virginian," p. 354.
9. *House Journal* 1877-78 "Governor's Annual Message" December 5, 1877.

Chapter 33

Return to Private Life

In December 1877, Kemper prepared to leave Richmond. He sorted wagon loads of papers in order to separate the public from the private and inventoried the contents of the mansion. He corresponded frequently with governor-elect Holliday during his final days in office.

January 1st, inauguration day, was clear and bright. Holliday's inauguration ceremony was elaborate, and included a long parade with a military escort. Kemper spoke a few words of farewell to the large crowd before he introduced his successor.[1]

Kemper and his children left Richmond almost immediately following the ceremony in a small wagon filled with his belongings and papers, followed by a pack of ponies, goats and dogs.[2] He wrote after leaving office, "I am down to hard-toil and hard-work, along with public life, done with politics, done with everything but toil and care for my family."[3] He returned to Richmond only rarely.

Kemper had given long and faithful service to his native state; now he had other obligations. He wrote:

---

1. Jones "Conservative Virginian," p. 366.
2. Seale.
3. Kemper to Nannie Tunstall, February 7, 1878.

For more than a quarter of a century, I gave to Virginia, in peace and war, the best that Nature gave me. Struck down and paralyzed in her service, knowing that others in ample numbers are abler to serve her than I am now, I act with a clear conscience in giving myself to the task of consolidating my domestic affairs—so long neglected—and achieving peace and repose for my declining years. . . . I have earned an honorable discharge.[4]

Numerous correspondents flooded Kemper with compliments on the way he had conducted his administration. He was often asked for his opinion and advice. He couldn't remain silent on important issues, especially the debt.

He took an active part on behalf of the Conservative Party in the summer of 1879. In October alone he spoke to rallies in fourteen counties and towns from King George to Bristol to Front Royal. Despite his efforts, the Conservatives lost big to the readjuster movement.[5]

The election of 1879 marked the end of Kemper's active participation in politics. Despite many pleas for his participation from the party, state and nation, Kemper retired permanently from public life. He did, however, continue to follow state and national politics closely, occasionally writing to the governor or Conservative Party leadership on important issues.[6]

He sought a mid-sized farm in a secluded area on which to retire and live a quiet life as a sheep farmer and eventually bought the 350-acre farm of C.L. Bankhead in Orange County for $10,000. The farm was named Edgemont, but it was commonly called the Punch Bowl for the bend in the Rapidan River; Kemper renamed it Walnut Hills.

---

4.   Kemper to F. W. M. Holliday, May 18, 1880.
5.   Jones "Conservative Virginian," pp. 374-377.
6.   *Ibid.*, p. 378.

There was a modest home on the property that had been completed in 1855 by the Bankheads,[7] but Kemper supervised construction of a large new mansion.

Walnut Hills stood on a high bluff overlooking the Rapidan River, with beautiful views of the Blue Ridge Mountains. The mansion had a long porch across the front with large bay windows. A conservatory and dining room were to the left of the large entry hall on the main floor, with a magnificent paneled library to the right. Upstairs were four large bedrooms, and above them a huge attic. The brick house had a low, shingled roof and four large chimneys, each marked with a cross on its broadest side. The interior was completed by a decorator from Richmond in the popular Victorian style.[8]

Walnut Hills had many service buildings, including a bathhouse, a windmill to draw water from the river, and a water-works or bubbling fountain in front of the mansion. Kemper also built a heated "Ellystic Pool," which he used for therapy. He would lounge in the warm water, often for hours at a time, to ease the pain in his legs. He confessed that he had built more extensively and expensively than wisely.[9]

While construction was going on at Walnut Hills, the children stayed with Miss Mora, Kemper's mother-in-law, in Madison. By the end of 1882 he had moved with his family to Orange County, having sold his interest in his law firm and his home in Madison to his old war comrade and law partner, Francis Marion McMullen, who was later a judge.[10]

---

7.   Ann L. Miller *Antebellum Orange: the Pre-Civil War Homes and Historic Sites of Orange County, Virginia* (Orange, Virginia, 1988) p. 110.
8.   Walnut Hills, although changed somewhat since Kemper lived there, is still basically the same. It is today the home of Mr. and Mrs. I. W. Jeannes.
9.   Jones "Conservative Virginian," p. 381.
10.   Captain McMullen continued to practice law in the small frame office and later was a circuit court judge for Madison and Greene counties. Mrs. McMullen operated a girls' school in the house, which remained in the McMullen family until 1962, when it was sold for use as an extension of Univ.

After the move, Kemper entered into a partnership with Judge James W. Morton. They shared a small frame law office in the yard of the clerk's office at Orange Court House. Kemper built a considerable practice in Madison, Orange, Greene and Culpeper counties, but by 1889 the pain from his wound forced him to retire from the practice of law.[11]

By far the most important item to Kemper at this point in his life was the welfare of his children. When the family moved to Walnut Hills, Kemper had six living children: Meade, 26; Florence (called Peggy), 21; James Jr., 18; Lucy, 14; Jessie, 13; and Heber, 11.[12]

Meade had straightened out his life after his escapades while he served as his father's secretary, and in 1878 graduated with honors from the Medical College of Richmond. In 1882 he married Alice Constance Taylor of Richmond, a classmate of his sister's. She died soon after the birth of their first and only child in 1883; their son died shortly thereafter. Meade, who was never in good health, died of heart failure in his office in Norfolk three years later. Meade, Alice and their son were all buried at Walnut Hills.[13]

Florence, the oldest girl, mothered the family. She took care of the younger children and handled the domestic duties. She was tutored at home, but attended Miss Gussie Daniel's school in Richmond for one year. She cared for her father until his death in 1895. Four years later, at the age of 38, she married John P. "Jack" Thompson of Orange County. They had no children. Together they operated Walnut Hills as a working farm and summer retreat.[14]

---

of Va. The McMullens are buried at Cedar Hill Cemetery. Judge McMullen's portrait hangs in the Madison County courthouse.

11.   Jones "Conservative Virginian," p. 382.

12.   Kemper and Wright *Genealogy*.

13.   Jones "Conservative Virginian," p. 382.

14.   From conversations with Mrs. Nancy DeJarnette (Thornton L.) Berry, whose family (the DeJarnettes of Orange County) bought Walnut Hills from Jack and Florence Thompson and personally knew them; and with Mr. and Mrs. I. W. Jeannes, the current owners of Walnut Hills.

James, Jr., attended Locust Dale Academy and Episcopal High School in Alexandria. He showed considerable ability but little ambition. There was no money to send him to college, so young James took a job with a commercial firm in Richmond following graduation. He took to heavy drinking, persuaded a Richmond merchant to give him $145 from his father's commission on the sale of some wheat, headed west and disappeared. After several years, Kemper hired the Pinkerton National Detective Agency to look for him. They tracked James to a poker game in St. Paul, where he had lost a large sum and again disappeared. Based upon the detective's conclusion that he was dead, either from suicide or murder, Kemper collected a $3,000 life insurance policy. James was not dead, however. Sometime around 1890 he turned up at Walnut Hills late at night, in a pouring rain, drunk. He was received only by the servants, Mammy and Uncle Jim, for Kemper refused to see him. He gave him some money and sent him on his way to Orange Court House in a farm carriage. Kemper had to return the insurance money, a serious financial burden. After this, the younger Kemper disappeared for good.[15]

Lucy and Jessie, only thirteen months apart in age, were close companions. They attended Powell School in Richmond from the fall of 1883 until the spring of 1886, and for most of 1886-1887 they traveled extensively, mostly visiting classmates. In the summer of 1887, Kemper sent Lucy on a grand tour of Europe for the improvement of her health. She married Dr. Junius F. Lynch in late 1891 and moved to Samford, Florida, following the birth of their only child, a daughter, Virginia Kemper Lynch, at Walnut Hills in 1893. The granddaughter was a delight to Kemper, who was overjoyed at the pleasure brought to him by having a child at Walnut Hills.[16]

Jessie lived a short, tragic life. She was engaged to marry Conway Sams of Baltimore, but fell ill at a mid-day meal shortly before

15.   *Ibid.*, Jones "Conservative Virginian," pp. 384-385.
16.   Jones "Conservative Virginian," p. 386.

her wedding and died within twenty-four hours, possibly of gall bladder trouble or acute appendicitis. She was buried in the small family plot at Walnut Hills.[17]

Heber, the youngest, was educated at the Mt. Welcome School at Mitchells Station, Virginia, and at the Hanover Academy, Bingham's School in North Carolina and the Eastern Business College in Poughkeepsie, New York. After holding a number of low-paying jobs in New York city, he saw distinguished service as a regimental scout in the U.S. Army in Cuba during the Spanish American war. He was later successful in business. His son, James Lawson, in the Kemper military tradition, graduated from the U.S. Naval Academy in 1932 and was killed in action during the second day of the great American naval victory at Guadalcanal, November 13, 1942. He held the rank of commander.[18]

Kemper spent his last few years with serious financial difficulties. Despite his reduced circumstances, he still lived as a Virginia gentleman, although not extravagantly. He continued to buy the finest tea and coffee and large quantities of whiskey, which he used as a pain killer. He owned a fine carriage, bought a piano for his girls, and kept a large number of ponies, horses and dogs.[19]

He often hosted gay parties. As the home of a former Confederate general and ex-governor, Walnut Hills was the center of social life in Orange County. Guests came from as far away as Richmond. Kemper was a strict father and a stern host. His daughters still were not permitted to dance a waltz, only reels and square dances, and the young gentlemen were asked to leave at 10:00 PM.[20]

The old general became quite religious in his later years. Although he never formally joined a church, he did regularly attend the Episcopal services in Orange.

---

17. *Ibid.*, p. 386.
18. *Ibid.*, p. 387.
19. *Ibid.*, p. 388.
20. Dunnington, p. 18; Jones "Conservative Virginian," p. 388.

Chapter 34

End of the Line

The last six years of the aging general's life were extremely difficult. Retired from his law practice, his income severely curtailed, he had to borrow to meet expenses, was stricken by serious illnesses and was injured in a number of incapacitating falls.

He wrote to his friend, R.L. Maury, in 1887:

My health is broken and my tenure of life is extremely precarious. For months I have lived in my room. My increasing paralysis is such that even with the help of crutches, I move with difficulty, pain, and hazard.[1]

A few months later he wrote to Nannie Tunstall:

What makes me melancholy is to remember the realities of my own life-status—the rapid whitening of my hair—my almost three-score years—my now painful progress through old age on crutches . . . —my sad struggle with debt after a long life of unflagging service and devotion to Virginia through peace and war![2]

---

1.   Kemper papers V.H.S., Kemper to R. L. Maury, April 7, 1887.
2.   *Ibid.*, Kemper to Nannie Tunstall, December 15, 1887.

By 1891 his condition had worsened a great deal. In another letter he wrote:

> I am a prostrate and a slowly dying man. A critically dangerous form of heart disease will soon end my life. . . . Under the best medical injunctions I am trying to prolong my poor life from day to day by deliberate inaction, by living in a state of quietude, seclusion, and profound repose. . . . [T]he receipt of a letter, and still more the sight of an unanswered letter on my table, affects me with heart-perturbation which is alarming.[3]

Because of his paralysis, he was barely able to move from one room to another in his home. In 1891 he wrote to Daniel A. Grimsley:

> For nearly five months I have not been able to get as far as from my bed and fire side . . . to my yard-gate. . . . My life's arrow is shot; the bow of such humble strength as I once had is unstrung forever. I have not the least hope of ever being able to leave my home alive.[4]

Kemper became a virtual recluse, seeing few visitors and rarely answering letters. He did, however, continue to take an active interest in the farm.[5] On December 14, 1892, he wrote to Bassett French:

> You talk of your difficulty of getting up when down. That is nothing. I must now be put to bed like a baby and after resting

---

3. *Ibid.*, Kemper to Delaware Kemper Hay, July 1891.
4. Kemper papers U.Va., Kemper to Daniel A. Grimsley, April 18, 1891.
5. *Ibid.*

there a day or more I must then be lifted up and dressed like a baby as my penalty for writing this letter. The storm has gone over me, and I lie like one of the old oaks scattered by the hurricane. I am torn up by the roots and lie prostrate there, I most unfeignedly recognize the Divine Justice.[6]

In a letter to his daughter Lucy he details his physical decline:

The disease of my shattered left hip is what the Scripture defines to be the "Rottenness of the bones." I cannot move the bones of that hip joint without suffering excruciating agony. If I turn over at night I am bound to scream. I cannot bear a particle of weight or pressure upon my left hip or leg. Its bones are hopelessly diseased. . . . Many nights I doubt if I can live till morning. God have mercy upon us miserable sinners.[7]

Less than two months before his death he informed Lucy of his poor financial condition:

Lucy, I am much poorer than any of my children seem to think I am. I depend solely upon this farm, and the crops of wheat and corn bring about half as much as formerly. The farm don't begin to pay its expenses. At the end of every month I have to worry in order to borrow enough to pay the wages of my farm-hands and house-hirelings, and so my debts are increasing. For several years I have not spent so much as one dollar upon my own clothing. When you write to Heber tell him that if he or James were here I could not possibly give either as much as fifty cents

---

6. Kemper papers V.H.S., Kemper to Bassett French, December 14, 1892.
7. Kemper papers U.Va., Kemper to Mrs. Junius F. Lynch, March 28, 1894.

in order to have a pair of shoes mended.[8]

The end was obviously near when Kemper wrote Dr. Moses D. Hogue in early April of 1895:

> I am so feeble, such a daily and constant sufferer, that I am rarely equal to the labor of even writing a letter. Not long ago, I measured 43 inches around my waist. Latterly my waist measure has been 56 inches, showing that what seems to be dropsical swelling has increased the girth of my body by more than a foot. But it is bronchitis and asthma that torture me worst both day and night. I often fear that I shall not live to see my dear little grand-child again.

Kemper added that he strove "not to repine" and to "bow to the will of God."[9] He did not see his grandchild again.

On Sunday, April 7, 1895, at ten o'clock in the evening, the 71-year-old former governor and Confederate general died. With only a simple ceremony to mark his passing, Kemper was laid to rest in the small family graveyard.[10]

The newspapers throughout the state lauded Kemper as the intrepid soldier, the great statesman, and the loyal friend, and declared that another link with the old South had been laid to rest. The Richmond *Dispatch* penned the words which Kemper might have appreciated most of all: "Virginia never had a more loving son, nor one that served her from more unselfish purposes."[11]

By the terms of Kemper's will, dated February 28, 1895, and probated in the Orange County circuit court on May 4, 1895, his missing son, James, Jr., was bequeathed $300 as a token of his fa-

---

8.   *Ibid.*, February 20, 1895.
9.   *Ibid.*, Kemper to Dr. Moses D. Hogue, April 9(?), 1895.
10. Later Florence and her husband were also buried there.
11. Richmond *Dispatch*, April 9, 1895.

ther's sympathy and blessing. This provision was made, Kemper said in the will, to satisfy his own mind. Florence received five-twelfths of the residue of the estate, Lucy four-twelfths, and Heber three-twelfths. The unequal divisions were necessary, Kemper explained, because his children had previously received unequal benefits from his estate.[12]

In 1905, Florence presented the Museum of the Confederacy in Richmond with her father's military frock coat and sword,[13] items still treasured in the collection of that museum.

Kemper's life defined the term "service to state." The contributions made by James Lawson Kemper to his native Virginia will forever be remembered.

---

12. Kemper's will recorded Orange County Circuit Court, Orange, Virginia.
13. *Catalogue of Uniforms: The Museum of the Confederacy* (Richmond, Virginia, 1987) pp. 31-32.

Bibliography and Sources

Books

Alexander, E. P. *Military Memoirs of a Confederate*. Bloomington, Indiana, 1962.

Bell, Robert T. *11th Virginia Infantry*. Lynchburg, Virginia, 1985.

Blake, Nelson M. *William Mahone of Virginia Soldier and Political Insurgent*. Richmond, 1935.

Boatner, Mark Mayo, III *The Civil War Dictionary*. New York, 1959.

Bridges, Hal *Lee's Maverick General: Daniel Harvey Hill*. New York, 1961.

Buchanan, Lamont *A Pictorial History of the Confederacy*. New York, 1951.

Bushong, Millard K. *Old Jube: A Biography of General Jubal A. Early*. Shippensburg, Pennsylvania, 1990.

Cappon, Lester Jesse *Bibliography of Virginia History Since 1865*. Charlottesville, 1930.

Clark, Champ *Gettysburg: The Confederate High Tide*. Alexandria, 1985.

Compton, E. H. *Reminiscences of Edward Howard Compton: A Survivor of Second Battle of Manassas and the Battle of Gettysburg*. Front Royal, Virginia, n.d.

Catton, Bruce *Never Call Retreat*. Garden City, New Jersey, 1965.

Cooke, John Easton *Wearing of the Gray: Being Personal Portraits, Scenes, and Adventures of the War*. New York, 1867.

Dabney, Virginius *The Last Review: The Confederate Reunion*, Richmond, 1932. Chapel Hill, North Carolina, 1984.

Davis, Burke *Gray Fox: Robert E. Lee and the Civil War*. New York, 1956.

Davis, Burke *They Called Him Stonewall: A Life of Lt. General T. J. Jackson, C.S.A.*. New York, 1988.

Davis, Burke *To Appomattox: Nine April Days 1865*. New York, 1959.

Davis, Margaret G. *Madison County, Virginia: A Revised History*. Madison, Virginia, 1977.

Davis, William C. *Battle at Bull Run: A History of the First Major Campaign of the Civil War*. Baton Rouge, 1977.

Davis, William C. *The Commanders of the Civil War*. New York, 1990.

Dickenson, Sally Bruce *Confederate Leaders*. Staunton, Virginia, 1937.

Dodson, E. Griffith *Speakers and Clerks of the Virginia House of Delegates 1776-1955*. Richmond, 1956.

Donald, David ed. *Divided We Fought: A Pictorial History of the War 1861-1865*. New York, 1952.

Dove, Vee *Madison County Homes and Family Heritages*. Kingsport, Tennessee, 1975.

Dowdey, Clifford *Death of a Nation: the Story of Lee and His Men at Gettysburg*. New York, 1958.

Dowdey, Clifford *Experiment in Rebellion*. Garden City, 1946.

Dowdey, Clifford *Lee*. Boston, 1965.

Dowdey, Clifford *Lee's Last Campaign: The Story of Lee and His Men Against Grant-1864*. New York, 1960.

Dowdey, Clifford *The Land They Fought For: The Story of the South as the Confederacy 1832-1865*. Garden City, New Jersey, 1955.

Dowdey, Clifford *The Seven Days: The Emergence of Lee*. Boston, 1964.

Dowdey, Clifford ed. *The Wartime Papers of R. E. Lee*. Boston, 1961.

Dunnington, Allen Gray *Forgotten as a Dream: Remembrances of a Virginia Lady*. Orange, Virginia, 1990.

Durkin, Joseph T. ed. John Dooley, *Confederate Soldier: His War Journal*. Notre Dame, Indiana, 1963.

Eaton, Clement *A History of the Southern Confederacy*. New York, 1954.

Eggleston, George A. *A Rebel's Recollections*. Bloomington, 1957.

Foote, Shelby *The Civil War: A Narrative (Fort Sumter to Perryville)*. New York, 1963.

Foote, Shelby *The Civil War: A Narrative (Fredericksburg to Meridian)*. New York, 1963.

Freeman, Douglas Southall *Lee's Lieutenants: A Study in Command*. New York, 1942.

Freeman, Douglas Southall *R. E. Lee: A Biography*. New York, 1945.

Gallagher, Gary W. *Fighting for the Confederacy: The Personal Recollections of General Edward Porter Alexander*. Chapel Hill, North Carolina, 1989.

Georg, Kathleen R. and Busey, John W. *Nothing But Glory: Pickett's Division at Gettysburg*. Hughestown, New Jersey, 1987.

Glasgow, William M., Jr. *Northern Virginia's Own*. Alexandria, Virginia, 1989.

Gordon, John Brown *Reminiscences of the Civil War*. New York, 1903.

Gray, John Chipman and Ropes, John Codman *War Letters 1862-1865 of John Chipman Gray: Major, Judge Advocate and John Codman Ropes: Historian of the War with Portraits*. Boston, 1927.

Gunn, Ralph White *24th Virginia Infantry*. Lynchburg, Virginia, 1987.

Hamlin, Percy Gatling *Old Bald Head (General R. S. Ewell) the Portrait of a Soldier*. Strasburg, Virginia, 1940.

Hamlin, Captain Percy Gatling, M.D., M.C., ed. *The Making of a Soldier: Letters of General R. S. Ewell*. Richmond, 1935.

Harrison, Walter *Pickett's Men: A Fragment of War History*. New York, 1870.

Hassler, William Woods *A. P. Hill: Lee's Forgotten General*. Richmond, 1957.

Henderson, G.F.R., Col. C.B. *Stonewall Jackson and the American Civil War*. New York, n.d.

Henry, Robert Selph *The Story of the Confederacy*. New York, 1931.

Hoehling, A. A. and Hoeling, Mary *The Last Days of the Confederacy: An Eyewitness Account of the Fall of Richmond, Capitol City of the Confederate States*. New York, 1981.

Hotchkiss, Jed ed. by Evans, Gen. Clement A. *Confederate Military History: Extended Edition Volume IV, Virginia*. Wilmington, North Carolina, 1987.

Hunter, Alexander *Johnny Reb and Billy Yank*. New York, 1905.

Johnson, David E. *Four Years a Soldier*. Charleston, 1887.

Johnson, David E. *The Story of a Confederate Boy in the Civil War*. Portland, Oregon, 1914.

Johnson, Robert Underwood and Buell, Clarence Clough ed. *Battles and Leaders of the Civil War*. Secaucus, New Jersey, 1956.

Johnson, Rossiter *Campfire and Battlefield: the Classic Illustrated History of the Civil War*. New York, 1978.

Johnson, Swafford *Great Battles of the Confederacy*. New York, 1985.

Jones, J. B. *A Rebel War Clerk's Diary at the Confederate States Capital*. Philadelphia, 1866.

Jones, Rev. J. William, D.D. *Christ in the Camp or Religion in Lee's Army*. Richmond, Virginia, 1888.

Kemper, James Lawson *A History of the Late Difficulties*. Washington, 1853.

Kemper, Willis Miller and Wright, Henry Lynn *Genealogy of the Kemper Family in the United States, Descendants of John Kemper of Virginia; with a Short Historical Sketch of His Family and of the German Reformed Colony at Germanna and Germantown, Virginia*. Chicago, 1899.

Lewis, Lieut. Richard *Camp Life of a Confederate Boy of Bratton's Brigade, Longstreet's Corps, C.S.A.*. Charleston, South Carolina, 1883.

Loehr, Charles T. *War History of the Old 1st Virginia Infantry Regiment, Army of Northern Virginia*. Richmond, 1884.

Maddox, Jack P. *The Virginia Conservatives 1867-1879: A Study in Reconstruction Politics.* Chapel Hill, North Carolina, 1970.

McLaughlin, Jack *Gettysburg: The Long Encampment, the Battle, the Men, the Memories.* New York, 1963.

McMurray, Richard M. Two Great Rebel Armies: An Essay in Confederate Military History. Chapel Hill, North Carolina, 1989.

Miller, Ann L. *Antebellum Orange: the Pre-Civil War Homes and Historic Sites of Orange County, Virginia.* Orange, Virginia, 1988.

Miller, Francis Travelyan *The Photographic History of the Civil War: The Armies and the Leaders.* New York, 1957.

Minnigh, L. W. Gettysburg: *What They Did Here.* Gettysburg, 1924.

Minor, Maria Williams *The Walkers of Woodberry Forest.* n.c., 1973.

Moger, Allen W. *Virginia: Bourbonism to Byrd 1870-1925.* Charlottesville, Virginia, 1968.

Moore, James Tice *Two Paths to the New South: The Virginia Debt Controversy 1870-1883.* Lexington, Kentucky, 1974.

Morgan, W. H. *Personal Reminiscences of the War of 1861-65.* Lynchburg, Virginia, 1911.

Murfin, James V. *The Gleam of Bayonets: The Battle of Antietam and the Maryland Campaign of 1862.* Baton Rouge, 1965.

Nofi, Albert A. *The Gettysburg Campaign: June and July 1863.* New York, 1986.

Pearson, C. C. *The Re adjuster Movement in Virginia.* New Haven, 1917.

Pickett, LaSalle Corbell *Pickett and His Men.* Philadelphia, 1913.

Piston, William Garnett *Lee's Tarnished Lieutenant: James Longstreet and His Place in Southern History.* Athens, Georgia, 1987.

Poague, William Thomas *Gunner with Stonewall: Reminiscences of William Thomas Poague.* Wilmington, 1957.

Powell, Col. Robert M. *Recollections of a Texas Colonel at Gettysburg.* Gettysburg, Pennsylvania, 1990.

Riggs, David *7th Virginia Infantry.* Lynchburg, Virginia, 1982.

Robertson, James I., Jr. *General A. P. Hill: The Story of a Confederate Warrior.* New York, 1987.

Salmon, Emily J. ed. *A Hornbook of Virginia History.* Richmond, 1983.

Schenck, Martin *Up Came Hill: The Story of the Light Division and Its Leaders.* Harrisburg, Pennsylvania, 1958.

Schwicht, Hermann *History of the German Element in Virginia.* Baltimore, 1989.

Scott, W. W. *A History of Orange County, Virginia.* Richmond, 1907.

Seale, William *Virginia's Executive Mansion.* Richmond, 1988.

Sears, Stephen W. *Landscape Turned Red: The Battle of Antietam.* New York, 1983.

Smith, William R. *The Diary of William Randolph Smith*. Manassas, Virginia, 1986.

Sorrell, G. Moxley *Recollections of a Confederate Staff Officer*. New York, 1905.

Stackpole, Edward J. *Drama on the Rappahannock: The Fredericksburg Campaign*. Harrisburg, Pennsylvania, 1957.

Stackpole, Edward J. *From Cedar Mountain to Antietam: August-September 1862: Cedar Mountain--Second Manassas--Chantilly--Harpers Ferry--South Mountain--Antietam*. Harrisburg, Pennsylvania, 1959.

Stackpole, Edward J. *They Met at Gettysburg*. New York, 1956.

Stewart, George R. *Pickett's Charge: A Microhistory of the Final Attack and Gettysburg, July 3, 1863*. Dayton, Ohio, 1983.

Thomas, William H. B. *Gordonsville, Virginia: Historic Crossroads Town*. *Orange*, Virginia, 1971.

Thomas, William H. B. *Orange, Virginia: Story of a Court House Town*. Orange, Virginia, 1972.

Thrift, George Nathaniel *A Reply*. Washington, 1854.

Tooke, Horne *Whose Overcoat Have You Got On?* New York, 1854.

Torpey, Dorothy M. *Hallowed Heritage: The Life of Virginia*. Richmond, 1961.

Tucker, Glenn *High Tide at Gettysburg: The Campaign in Pennsylvania*. Dayton, Ohio, 1983.

Wallace, Lee A., Jr. *A Guide to Virginia Military Organizations 1861-65*. Lynchburg, Virginia, 1986.

Wallace, Lee A., Jr. *1st Virginia Infantry*. Lynchburg, Virginia, 1985.

Wallace, Lee A., Jr. *3rd Virginia Infantry*. Lynchburg, Virginia, 1986.

Wallace, Lee A., Jr. *17th Virginia Infantry*. Lynchburg, Virginia, 1990.

Warfield, Edgar *A Confederate Soldier's Memoirs*. Richmond, 1936.

Warner, Ezra J. *Generals In Gray: The Lives of the Confederate Commanders*. Baton Rouge, 1959.

Williams, T. Harry *P.G.T. Beauregard: Napoleon in Gray*. Baton Rouge, 1955.

Woodward, C. Vann ed. *Mary Chestnut's Civil War*. New Haven, 1981.

Woodward, Harold R., Jr. *For Home and Honor: the Story of Madison County, Virginia During the War Between the States 1861-65*. Madison, Virginia, 1990.

Wynes, Charles E. *Race Relations in Virginia 1870-1902*. Charlottesville, Virginia, 1961.

Younger, Edward ed. *Inside the Confederate Government: The Diary of Robert Gaslick Hill Kean, Head of the Bureau of War*. New York, 1957.

Younger, Edward *The Governors of Virginia 1860-1978*. Charlottesville,

Virginia, 1982.

Yowell, Claude Lindsay I Strasburg, Virginia, 1926.

n.a. *Catalogue of Uniforms: The Museum of the Confederacy.* Richmond, Virginia, 1987.

n.a. *Great Battles of the Civil War.* New York, 1989.

n.a. *Lee Takes Command: From Seven Days to Second Bull Run.* Alexandria, Virginia, 1984.

n.a. *Orange Court House 1861-1865.* Orange, Virginia, 1961.

Theses and Dissertations

"A Historical Survey of Changes in Education in Madison County 1792-1970" by John Edward Dwyer, master thesis, University of Richmond, 1970.

"Conservative Virginian: The Postwar Career of James Lawson Kemper" by Robert Rivers Jones, Ph.D. dissertation, University of Virginia, 1964.

"Forgotten Virginian: The Early Life and Career of James Lawson Kemper, 1823-1865" by Robert Rivers Jones, master thesis, University of Virginia, 1961.

"The 7th Virginia Infantry Regiment, C.S.A." by Louis Ford Hitt, master thesis, Virginia Polytechnic Institute and State University, 1972.

Letters and Papers

Fact Sheet Kemper Mansion, prepared by Jan Harris, Madison Heritage Foundation, Madison, Virginia.

James Lawson Kemper Information, Madison Heritage Foundation, Madison, Virginia.

Kemper Family File, Albemarle County Historical Society, Charlottesville, Virginia.

Kemper File, Orange County Historical Society, Orange, Virginia.

Letter from Kemper's Brigade to Mayor of Fredericksburg, National Park Service, Fredericksburg National Military Park.

Letter of James Lawson Kemper, Steven S. Hoffman, Brightwood, Virginia.

Papers of James Lawson Kemper, University of Virginia Library, Charlottesville, Virginia.

Papers of James Lawson Kemper, Virginia Historical Society, Richmond, Virginia.

Papers of James Lawson Kemper, Virginia State Library, Richmond, Virginia.

Records of the Fishback Wagon Factory, Steven S. Hoffman, Brightwood, Virginia.

Official Manuscripts

Acts of the Virginia General Assembly 1859-60.
Collection of the National Archives.
Journal of the Virginia House of Delegates 1853-54; 1855-56; 1859-60; 1861-62; 1873-74; 1874-75; 1875-76; 1876-77; 1877-78.
Journal of the Virginia Senate 1873-74; 1874-75; 1875-76; 1876-77; 1877-78.
Register of the General Assembly.
"War of the Rebellion: A Compilation of the Official Records of the Union and Confederate Armies," 128 vol., Washington, D.C., 1880-1891, U.S. War Department.

Newspaper Articles

Madison County *Eagle,* October 26, 1961.
Richmond *Dispatch,* August 16, 1873; August 26, 1873; October 25, 1873; January 2, 1874; April 9, 1895.
Richmond *Enquirer,* October 27, 1875.
Staunton *Spectator,* December 30, 1873.
Washington Daily National Intelligencer, January 4, 1847.

Magazine Articles

"A Gallant Defense: Gettysburg Combat" by Martin Graham *Civil War Times Illustrated* vol. XXV no. 3 May 1986, p. 12.
"A Private in the 11th Virginia Infantry Regiment" by Joan Logan Brooks *The United Daughters of the Confederacy Magazine* vol. LIV March 1991, no. 3, p. 24.
"Courthouses of Madison County" by William H. B. Thomas *Virginia Calvacade* vol. XIX no. 4 Spring 1970, p. 16.
"Foraging South of the James River: General James Longstreet's Suffolk Campaign Revisited" *Confederate Veteran* March-April 1991, p. 14.
"Henry A. Wise and the Campaign of 1873: Some Selected Letters from the Papers of James Lawson Kemper," edited by James A. Bern, Jr. *Virginia Magazine of History and Biography* vol. 62 No. 3 July 1954, p. 321.
"Longstreet Takes Command" by Theodore P. Savas *America's Civil War* March 1990, p. 35.
"J. L. Kemper and the Virginia Redeemers Face the Race Question: A Reconsideration" by R. R. Jones *Journal of Southern History* vol. 30 1972, pp. 393-414.

"Nothing But Glory Gained" by Robert C. Checks *America's Civil War* September 1990, p. 32.

"Pickett's Charge and Numerous Countercharges" by Kent Masterson Brown *Virginia Country's Civil War Quarterly* vol. II, p. 36.

"Please Don't Make Me a General in the Confederate Army!" by Richard F. Selcer *Civil War* vol. XIX, p. 48.

"Return to the Killing Ground" by Jeffrey D. West *America's Civil War* July 1991, p. 18.

"Siege of Suffolk 1863: Another Name for Futility?" by W. Glenn Robertson *Virginia Calvacade* vol. XXVII no. 4 Spring 1978, p. 164.

"The Gray Ghost in Mofti: The Postwar Career of John S. Mosby" by Kevin H. Siepel *Virginia Calvacade* vol. 36 no. 2 Autumn 1986, p. 74.

"The Long Fight Over the Bloody Angle" by Daniel Bauer *Civil War* vol. XVII, p. 37.

"The Master General: 'It's All My Fault,' Taking the Blame at Gettysburg" by Mark Grimsley *Civil War Times Illustrated* vol. XXIV no. 7 November 1985, p. 38.

"The Mexican War Diary of James Lawson Kemper" by Robert R. Jones *The Virginia Magazine of History and Biography* vol. 74 no. 4 October 1966, p. 387.

"The South's Last Boys in Gray: James Albert Spicer" by Professor Jay S. Hoar *Confederate Veteran* November-December 1990, p. 39.

"The Third Day at Gettysburg" by Frank Aretas Haskell *American Heritage: The Magazine of History* December 1957, vol IX, No. 1, p. 30.

Tyler's Quarterly Historical and Genealogical Magazine, vol. VI No. 1 July 1924, p. 72.

Tyler's Quarterly Historical and Genealogical Magazine, vol. VII No. 3 January 1925, p. 158.

Virginia Country's Civil War Quarterly vol. IX.

William and Mary College Quarterly Historical Magazine, No. 1 vol. III July 1894.

"William 'Extra Billy' Smith, Governor of Virginia 1864-65, A Pillar of the Confederacy" by Alvin A. Fahrer *The Virginia Magazine of History and Biography* vol. 74 no. 1 January 1966, p. 71.

Unpublished Works

"The Blue Ridge Turnpike Story" by Harold R. Woodward, Jr.

"The History of the Militia in Madison County 1724-Present" by Sgt. Harold R. Woodward, Jr.

Index

1st Brigade (Va. Militia)   27
1st Brigade (Kemper's)   57-101 *passim*
1st Virginia   8, 9, 11, 43, 46, 53, 56,
    59, 68-69, 70, 72, 74, 76-77, 80, 87,
    89, 91, 107, 178
2nd Brigade (Garnett's)   72, 87
2nd Michigan   48
3rd Brigade (Armistead's)   72, 87
3rd Virginia   73, 76-77, 87, 89, 107
4th Brigade   (Longstreet's Div.) 46;
    (Pickett's Div.) 73-74
IV Corps   54
4th Virginia Cavalry   111
5th Texas Infantry   102
VI Corps   115
7th Louisiana   40, 43, 44
7th Virginia   36, 37-46, 47-48, 50-51,
    52-56, 57, 59, 60, 65-68, 69, 72,
    76-77, 80, 81, 87, 89, 91, 107; Co.
    A 37, 80; B 37, 39, 48, 91; C 38; D
    38, 39, 48, 53; E 38; F 38; G 37; H
    38, 39; I 38, 39; K 37, 39, 48; regi-
    mental band 85
8th Virginia   72, 96
9th New York   69-70
9th Virginia   72
11th Pennsylvania   66, 71
11th Virginia   46, 52, 56, 59, 63, 68-
    69, 72, 77, 87, 89, 107; Co. C 96;
    Co. H 89
13th Mississippi   42, 44
14th Virginia   72, 101
15th Virginia   74
17th Virginia   46, 52, 56, 59, 60, 63,
    66, 68-69, 71, 72, 74, 78, 107; Co.
    A 80
18th Virginia   72

19th Mississippi   53
19th Virginia   72, 82, 111
24th North Carolina   74
24th Virginia   39, 40, 56, 59, 65, 68,
    69, 72, 77, 81, 87, 89, 94, 100, 107;
    Co. B 66
28th Virginia   72
29th Virginia   74
30th Virginia   74
32nd Virginia   74
38th Virginia   72
49th Virginia   37
53rd Virginia   72
56th Virginia   72, 82
57th Virginia   72
103rd New York   71

——, Mammy   189
——, Oliver   163, 170
——, Sam   47
——, Uncle Jim   189

A

Adams Express Co.   125
Alexander, E. Porter   60, 90, 92
Allison, John Stadler   2
Allison, Mary Dorothea Stadler (grand-
    mother)   2
Allison, Thomas Lawson (grandfa-
    ther)   2
Almond, J.W.   38
American Industrial Agency   125
amnesty oath   121
Anderson, Joseph R.   125
Anderson, Richard H.   63
Anderson, Robert   39n
Appomattox Court House   114

Archer, James J. 61
Armistead, A.D. 130
Armistead, Lewis 72, 87, 94, 96-97, 98, 100
Army of Northern Virginia 57, 83, 113
Army of the Potomac 73
Ashby, Philip S. 67, 69
Athey, W.W. 71
Atlantic, Mississippi and Ohio RR 141
Augusta County, Va. 7
Aylett, Patrick Henry 12

B

Bagby, Thomas H. 10
Baldwin, John B. 134, 136, 140
Baltimore and Ohio Railroad 141
Bankhead, C.L. 186
Banks, Lynn 27
Banks, Robert Adam 18, 22, 27, 30, 120, 123, 136
Banks, William E. 131
Barbour, James 126, 136, 140, 141, 148, 165
Barbour, John S. 18, 28, 49, 126, 152
Barksdale, William 44, 74
Barton, Seth M. 125, 126
battle flag (Confederate) 49
battles
    Boonsborough (Boonsboro) 67-68
    Buena Vista (Mex. War) 13
    Chancellorsville 82
    Frayser's farm 59-61
    Fredericksburg 74-77
    Gaines's Mill 58-59, 61, 72
    Gettysburg 86-100, 102, 104
    Malvern Hill 61
    Manassas (1st) 15, 42-45, 47
    Manassas (2nd) 65-67, 71
    Mechanicsville 58
    New Market 109
    Seven Pines 54-56, 67, 159
    Sharpsburg 68-71
    Williamsburg 52-53
Beauregard, P.G.T. 34, 40-45, 47, 48, 49, 50

Beazley, Robert S. 135
Beazley, Wyatt 145
Bedinger, Henry 10
Belcher, Charles 100
Bell, John 31, 134
Berkley, Edmund 96
Bingham's School 190
Blackburn's Ford (engagement) 42-44
Blackford, Charles M. 88
Blair, Francis P. 140
Blakey, Angus R. 22, 33
Blue Ridge Turnpike Co. 17-18
Bocock, John Holmes 1n, 40, 105
Bocock, Sarah Margaret Kemper 1n, 106, 115
Bocock, Thomas S. 136, 140, 153, 156, 157
Bonham, M.L. 41
Booton, Edwin 126
Botts, Maria Rebecca Kemper 1n
Botts, William F. 1n, 102
bounties (re-enlistment) 49
bounty claims (Mexican War) 17
Bouton, George 147
Bragg, Braxton 14, 109
Branch, Lawrence O. 61
Bream, Francis 101
Breckenridge, John C. 31, 112
Bright, Robert A. 92-93, 100
Brock, R.A. 95-96
Brown, Benjamin 148
Brown, John 27-28
Brown, William A. 91
Buchanan, James 11, 26, 30, 31
Bucktails 146, 151
Burnside, Ambrose 69, 70, 73, 75

C

Calhoun, John Caldwell 11
Call, James 153
Camp Walker 42
Camp Wigfall 38, 40
Carter, Dale 134
Carter house 45
Casey, Silas 54
Castle Thunder 110

Cave, Belfield 18, 22, 118
Cave, Benjamin 163
Cave, Cremora 67, 118, 164, 187
Cave, Cremora Conway (see Kemper, Belle)
Cedar Grove plantation 2
Cedar Mountain 63
Chamberlayne, J. Hampden 153
Chambersburg and Harrisburg RR 86
Chambersburg, Pa. 85
Chandler house 82
Chapman, Augustus Alexander 10
Charleston, W. Va. 7
Chesapeake and Ohio RR 145, 182-183
Chestnut, James R. 50
Chestnut, Mary 111
Chinn house 66
Cincinnati School of Military Science 7
civil rights 166-168, 181
Clark's farm 54
Cleary, William 38
Clement, Adam 63
Cobb, Howell 134
Cochran, Alexander B. 168
Cocke, Philip St. George 15, 36, 45
Codori house 94, 95, 96
Codori, Nicholas 94
Cole, —— 126
Coleman, Samuel S. 71
Coleman, W.D. 169
College of William and Mary 52
Colston, Raleigh 53
Colt Patented Firearms Co. 34
Compton, Edward Howard 91, 93, 97
Confederate States of America 32, 36
Conscription Act 108, 109
Conservative Party 136, 139, 141, 144, 145, 146, 147, 148, 149, 150, 152, 155-156, 157, 160-161, 164, 180, 183, 186
Constitutional Union Party 31
Conway, B.T.F. 123
Conway, T.S. 123-124
Cooper, Samuel 41, 110

Corse, Montgomery D. 56, 63, 65-66, 73-74, 82, 84
Crisler, Norman 40, 45-46

D

Dabney, William Pope 150
Daniel, Augusta (Gussie) 163, 188
Daniel, Raleigh T. 136, 153, 157
Daniels, —— (U.S.A) 95
Danville 114, 138
Davidson, E.M. 183
Davis, Jefferson 14, 32, 50, 55, 82, 113, 114, 115, 121, 177
de Grafenuid, Baron 2
Democratic Party 18, 24, 26, 30, 31, 134, 139, 140, 150, 155, 161
DeNormandie, Lucile Amelia (see Kemper, Lucile Amelie DeNormandie)
Dept. of Virginia and North Carolina 79
detailed men 108
Dimmock, —— 50
Dispatch 165, 194
Dooley, James H. 174
Dooley, John 70, 91, 124
Dorman, Charles 10
Douglas, Henry Kydd 102
Douglas, Stephen 12, 30, 31
Drayton, Thomas F. 65
Drinkard, W.F. 154
Drogan house 45
Duke, Basil 134
Dunnington, C.W.C. 134

E

Early, Jubal Anderson 12, 40, 42, 44, 43, 45, 46, 49, 153, 156, 165, 177-178
Earnest, J. 19
Eastern Business College 190
Eastern Hospital for the Insane 52
Echols, John 124
Edgemont 186
Ellystic Pool 187
Elzey, Arnold 44, 82

Eubank, John   177
Evans, Nathan 'Shanks'   65-66
Ewell, Richard   49, 50, 51, 82, 113
Exact (steamer)   12
Examiner   158
Exchange Hotel   157

F

Field, Charles W.   134
Field, James G.   148, 163, 183
Field, Richard H.   21
Fillmore, Millard   134
First National flag   48-49
Fitzhugh, E.H.   165
Flournoy, Thomas S.   24, 136
Floweree, Charles C.   40, 51, 53, 66, 79
Foley, J.H.   177
Forrest, French   82
Fort McHenry   103
Fort Sumter   34, 39n
Fortress Monroe   9, 12, 14, 104
Frayser's farm (see battle of)
Fredericksburg   77
Fredericksburg and Gordonsville RR   145
free railroad law   146
Freeman, Arthur   1n
Freeman, Mary Allison Kemper   1n, 119
French, S. Bassett   147, 192-193
Fry, Birkett Davenport   9
Fry, Thomas V.   80
Fry, William O.   120, 129, 141
Fultz, David   155
Funders   144
Funding Act of 1871   146, 173, 174
Funsten, David   56, 63

G

Garland, Samuel   56
Garnett, Richard Brooke   68, 72, 82, 87, 94, 96, 98, 99, 100
Garrett, John   141
Gates, Theodore   95
Geiger, George E.   96

Germanna colony   2
Gibson, Eustace   39
Gibson, J. Catlett   37
Glazebrook, L.W.   124
Goggin, W.L.   27
Goode, John   134, 141
Goss, Ebenezer   110-111
Graham, Charles K.   104
Grant, Ulysses S.   112, 113, 114, 140, 150, 164-165, 166, 169, 170
Graves, A.W.   134, 136
Graves v. Early   20-22
Greeley, Horace   148, 149
Green, J.W.   40
Grimsley, Daniel A.   147, 192

H

Hairston, George   39
Halifax County   115
Hall, N.J.   95
Hambrick, Joseph   66
Hammer, George   96
Hamtramck, John   12, 13-14
Hancock, Winfield Scott   181
Hanover Academy   190
Harman, Michael   124
Harpers Ferry federal arsenal   27-28
Harrison, Walter   125
Harrow, William   95
Hart, Benjamin   124
Hay, Delaware Kemper   192n
Hayes, Rutherford B.   181, 183
Hayes, Mrs. R.B.   183
Hays, Henry T.   40, 44
Hazelwood Volunteers   38, 39
Hermitage Cup   183
Heth, Henry   87, 177
Heth, Mrs. Henry   164
Hewson, M. Butt   134
Hill, Ambrose Powell   4, 35, 49, 50-51, 52-53, 58, 63, 70, 82
Hill, D.H.   68
Hill, Henry   4, 9
Hogue, Moses D.   178, 194
Hoke, Robert F.   134
Holcombe Guards   38, 39

Holliday, F.W.M.   183, 185
Hollywood Cemetery   179
Hood, John Bell   58, 63, 65
Hope, Beresford   183
Hopewell meeting house   71
Houston, Sam   12
Howard's Grove   54
Hubbard, Edmund Wilcox   10
Hughes, Robert W.   151, 155, 157-
   158, 161
Hulter, James R.   89
Humphreys, Benjamin G.   134
Humphreys, Thomas Jefferson   30
Hundley, George   167
Hunter, Alexander   66, 69
Hunter, David   109
Hunter, Robert M.T.   12, 134, 136,
   157, 170, 174
Hunton, Eppa   65-66, 96, 148, 156

I

Imboden, John D.   7, 86, 124, 125,
   129, 180-181

J

Jackman, Sidney D.   125
Jackson, Julia   177
Jackson, Mrs. T.J.   177, 178
Jackson, Thomas J. "Stonewall"   50,
   51, 63-64, 65, 68, 70, 82, 177, 178,
   183
Jackson-Hope medal   183
James River and Kanawha Canal   155-
   156, 176, 179, 183
Jenkins, Micah   61, 65-66, 74, 84
Johnson, Andrew   119, 120, 121
Johnson, David E.   60, 99
Johnston, Joseph Eggleston   11, 44,
   48, 49, 50, 54, 55, 114, 124, 177,
   178
Johnston, David E.   91
Jones, Catesby ap. R.   125
Jones, David R.   44, 63, 65-66, 67

K

Kelley, A.M.   157
Kemper, Alice Constance Taylor   19n,
   188
Kemper, Ann Löw   1
Kemper, Belle   18, 27, 102, 103, 118,
   119, 131, 146
Kemper, Cremora Conway Cave (see
   Kemper, Belle)
Kemper, Florence "Peggy"   (see
   Thompson, Florence Kemper)
Kemper, Frances Merriweather   19n,
   105
Kemper, Frederick (grandfather)   2
Kemper, Frederick Thomas (brother)   1n, 119, 147
Kemper James Lawson
   ancestors 1-2; attorney 16-19; Blue
   Ridge Turnpike Co. 17-18; brigade
   commander 55, 72-78; campaigns
   for governor 155-160; carriage accident 148; children 19n, 130-131,
   163, 179, 185, 188-190; civil rights
   135; commands reserve forces 107-
   113; commissioned Va. militia 10-
   11; death 194; considered for
   governor 149-154; debate with
   Hughes 157-158; division commander 63; education 4, 5, 6-8; elected
   governor 161; enters politics 18;
   farewell speech (as governor) 184;
   founds Madison Acad. 130; governor 165-184; health 17, 36, 49, 106,
   115, 128-129, 132, 183-184, 191-
   193, 194; House of Delegates 22-
   23, 24-26, 27, 28-29, 49-50;
   improves military preparedness in
   Va. 28-29, 33-36, 47; inauguration
   165; marries 19; Mexican War service 13-14; pall bearer for Jackson
   82; petitions for pardon 121-122;
   post-war business ventures 123-
   127; post-war debts 117; prison of
   war 102-103; promoted to major
   general 110; quartermaster for
   Beauregard 40, 41; religion 27, 190;

resumes law practice 128-130; retires to Walnut Hills 186-190; retreats to Danville 114-115; siblings 1, 1n, 119; Speaker of House 49; surrenders, 115; threat of duel 21; urges emancipation 112; U.S. Army service 10-15; V.M.I. board of visitors 26; widowed 131; wounded 98, 100-101, 105

Kemper, James Lawson (grandson) 190, 193

Kemper, James Lawson, Jr. 19n, 188, 189, 195

Kemper, Jessie McRae 19n, 188, 189-190

Kemper, Johann 1

Kemper, John 1

Kemper, John George 1

Kemper, John Peter 2

Kemper, John Stadler (brother) 1n, 21, 102, 119

Kemper Kampaign Klub 160, 161, 165

Kemper, Lucile Amelia DeNormandie 19n

Kemper, Lucy Virginia (see Lynch, Lucy Virginia Kemper)

Kemper, Maria E. Allison (mother) 1, 2-3, 4, 64, 119

Kemper, Maria Rebecca (see Botts, Maria Rebecca Kemper)

Kemper, Mary Allison (see Freeman, Mary Allison Kemper)

Kemper, Meade Cave 19n, 130, 131, 147, 164, 165, 180, 188

Kemper, Reginald Heber Johns 19n, 131, 188, 190, 193, 195

Kemper, Sarah Margaret (see Bocock, Sarah Margaret Kemper)

Kemper, Susan Elizabeth (see Matthews, Susan Elizabeth Kemper)

Kemper, Susan Holt Taylor 1n

Kemper, William (father) 1, 2, 3, 4, 19

Kemper, William Henry 1n

Keys, Erasmus 54

Kinderhook farm 129

Kirkland, William Lennow 111

Know-Nothing Party 24, 31, 139, 150

L

Lang, James Henry 95

Leake, Shelton F. 9, 12, 22, 24

Lee, Fitzhugh 156, 177, 183

Lee, George Washington Custis 107

Lee, Robert E. 28, 35, 55, 58, 62, 63, 67, 73, 77, 81, 84, 85-86, 89, 93, 100-101, 102, 106, 107, 109, 111, 113, 114, 121, 122

Letcher, John 7, 27, 28, 32, 34n, 35, 82, 136, 159

Lincoln, Abraham 31, 34, 73, 114, 119

Locust Dale Academy 5, 130, 189

Loehr, Charles T. 56

Longstreet, James 42, 43, 44, 49, 53, 55, 57, 60-61, 63, 64, 66-67, 68, 71, 74, 76, 81, 82, 86, 92, 93

Lovell, William 37, 48

Lynch, Junius F. 19n, 189

Lynch, Lucy Virginia Kemper 19n, 188, 189, 193, 195

Lynch, Virginia Kemper 19n, 189, 194

Lynchburg 138

Lynn Banks Masonic Lodge 27

M

Madison Academy 130-131

Madison County 2, 28, 33, 35, 37, 38, 46, 118-120, 129, 130, 133, 135, 139, 145n, 146, 147, 148

Madison Grays 37, 39

Magruder, John B. 51

Mahone, William 140-141, 146, 150, 151-152, 153, 157, 158, 183

March, William L. 10

Marye, Jr. John L. 139

Marye, Morton 63

Maryland Campaign 67-71

"Maryland, My Maryland" 67

Mason, James Murray 12

Mason, John Y.   9
Mason-Dixon line   85
Massie, Thomas B.   37, 39
Matthews house   45
Matthews, Oliver   1n
Matthews, Susan Elizabeth Kemper   1n, 119
Maury, R.L.   191
Mayo, Jr., Joseph   73, 89, 100, 151, 153, 157, 169, 170
Mays, —— (7th Va. color bearer)   53
McCarthey, Florence M.   40
McClellan, George B.   50, 54, 59, 64, 68, 73
McCready, N.T.   158
McCue, John H.   7
McDonald, James   170
McDowell, Irwin   14
McDowell, James   10
McGilvery, Freeman   94, 95
McLean farm   42, 43
McLean, Nathan C.   66
McMullen, Francis Marion   38, 147, 187
Meade, George   86, 101-102
Meade, N.B.   151, 157
Mexican War   8, 13-15, 17
Miles, D.H.   115
Miles, William P.   50
Military District I   135, 144
Militia Act of 1860   29
Moffitt, Samuel H.   153, 167
Montague, R.L.   27, 153
Moore, Patrick T.   108, 121, 123, 124
Moore, Sam   148
Morgan, W.H.   80
Morton, C.B.   40
Morton, James W.   188
Mosby, John S.   156, 165, 169
Mt. Welcome School   190
Mountain Boomers   38, 39
Mountain Prospect   1, 3-4, 7
Museum of the Confederacy   195

N

Narrow Gauge Railway Co.   145-146

National Express and Transportation Co.   124-125
"New Movement"   140
New York Southern Lands Co.   125
Newman, Marcus   18, 19, 24
Norfolk and Petersburg Railroad   140
Norris, Richard   103
North Carolina Campaign   79-81

O

observation balloon   48
Old Field School   4
Orange and Alexandria Railroad   23, 126, 141, 145
Ordinance of Secession   34, 35, 36
Otey, Kirkwood   89
Ould, Robert   103, 157
overcoat feud   20-22

P

Patton, Waller Tazewell   40, 48, 51, 53, 54, 56, 81, 89
Payne, William H.   125
Peace Convention   32
Pendleton, A.G.   134
Pennsylvania Campaign   84-102
Pennsylvania Central   145, 146, 150
Petersburg   111, 113, 166-168, 169, 181, 182
Petersburg Railroad   79, 80
Pettigrew, J.J.   87
Pettit, John   12
Pickett, George E.   61, 71, 72, 74, 76, 78, 82, 84, 86, 89, 92, 93, 100, 107, 179
Pickett's Charge   94-98
Piedmont Agricultural Society   147
Pierce, Franklin   134
Pierpoint, Francis H.   119, 120-121, 170
Pinkerton Nat'l Detective Agency   189
plantation life   3-4
Platt, James H.   169
Polk, James   8, 10, 11
Pollock, Thomas Gordon   96
pontoon bridge   59, 74

Pope, John 62, 63, 64, 65
Porter, C.B. 152
Porter, John C. 38
Poell, Paulus 18
Powell, Robert M. 102
Powell School 189
Powhatan (steamer) 10
Powhatan House (hotel) 10, 22
Preston, John S. 112
Proclamation of Pardon 120
Provisional Army of the Confederate
  States 36
Provisional Army of Virginia 35, 36
Pryor, Roger A. 50, 73
Pryor, Theodore 83
Punch Bowl 186
Purcell, Charles W. 124

R

Radical Party 133, 135, 139, 140,
  141, 155, 161
Ramsdell, C.P. 155
Randolph, Thomas Jefferson 136
Ransom, Robert 74
Rappahannock Guard 37
Readjusters 144
Reconstruction Act 135, 180
Republican Party 31, 140, 155-156,
  158, 166
Rhett, Robert Barnwell 12
Richardson, Israel B. 42
Richardson, William H. 10, 25-26, 46,
  134, 145, 152, 156, 163
Richardson's Guards 28, 37, 38
Richmond, fall of 115
Richmond and Danville RR 146
Richmond and Petersburg RR 146
Richmond *Dispatch* 165, 194
Richmond *Enquirer* 178
Richmond *Examiner* 158
Richmond, Frederick and Potomac RR
  146
Richmond Grays 10
Richmond *Whig* 151, 160
Ripley, R.S. 111
Rittenhouse, Benjamin 94

Rives, George E. 153
Robinson, J.M. 158
Rogers, Arthur 65
Rorty, J.M. 95
Rosser, Thomas L. 124
Rutherford, John C. 7

S

Sams, Conway 189
Schofield 139
Schofield, John M. 135
Scott, —— (capt. Richmond
  Grays) 10
Scott, John 165, 169
secession 28, 31-32, 35
Seddon, James Alexander 10, 112
servants, Mammy and Uncle Jim 189
Seven Days Campaign 52-61
Seymour, Horatio 140
Shackelford, Henry G. 18, 145
Sheridan, Philip 109
Shields, J.C. 151
Skinner, Frederick G. 56
Slaughter, James E. 12
slavery 11-12, 19, 28, 112, 119, 121,
  136
Smith, G.W. 54
Smith, William "Extra Billy" 10, 114,
  120, 141, 156
Smoot, Thomas 136
snowball fight 78, 80
Southern Democratic Party 30, 31
Southern Express Co. 124
Southside Consolidation Act 146
Southside Railroad 109, 140
Sperryville Sharpshooters 37
Spotswood, Alexander 2
spy 64
Stadler, John Jasper 2
Stannard, George 95
Staples, Waller R. 151
States, The 134
states' rights 12, 19, 25, 139
Staunton 138
Stephens, Alexander H. 32, 134, 168
Stewart, J.E. 157

212

Stoneman, George 129
Stringfellow, Charles S. 153
Strother, John R. 147
Strother, L.H. 183
Stuart, Alexander H.H. 133, 136, 140
Stuart, James E.B. (Jeb) 15, 28, 44, 66
Summers, George W. 7-8
surrender 114

T

Taliaferro, William B. 147, 177, 183
Tansill, George S. 40
Taylor, Alice Constance (see Kemper, Alice Taylor)
Taylor, J.W. 131
Taylor, John 38
Taylor, Zachary 14
Tee-Total Society 7
Terry 96, 107
Terry, William R. 40, 56, 96, 107
Thomas, Henry W. 168, 174
Thompson, Florence Kemper 19n, 131, 188, 195
Thompson, John (Jack) P. 19n, 188
Thrift, George Nathaniel 20-22, 24
Tilden, Samuel J. 181
Tooke, Horne 22
Toombs, Robert A. 11, 69, 78
Treadway, William Marshall 10
Tredegar Iron Works 125
Trent affair 12
Trimble, Isaac R. 87, 102
True Republican Party 141
Tucker, John Randolph 136
Tunstall, Nannie 191
Twyman, James W. 39
Tyler, John 32
Tyler, Jr., John 125

U

U.S. Army Gen. Hospital (Baltimore) 103
U.S. centennial celebration 180-181
Underwood constitution 139, 169, 179
Underwood, John C. 139

V

Virginia, commonwealth of
board of immigration, 177; joins C.S.A. 36; Military District I 135; post-war debt, 143-145; 172-174; 182; post-war economy, 123, 137-138; restored to Union, 140, 141; state seals replaced, 170
Virginia and Tennessee Railroad 140
Virginia Central Railroad 38, 64
Virginia Military Institute 7, 26, 29, 36, 109, 110, 183
Virginia militia 24-25, 26, 28-29, 33-36, 47

W

Walden, Austin J. 37
Walker, George 96
Walker, Gilbert C. 141, 142, 143, 145, 146, 147, 148, 150, 151, 157, 163, 164, 165, 166, 169
Walker, James A. 139, 1531, 183
Walker, James W. Jr. 141
Walker, Samuel H. 11
Wallace, H.N. 46
Wallace, Thomas P. 136
Walnut Hills 19n, 186-187, 188, 189, 190
War of 1812 17
Washington Artillery (Louisiana) 42
Washington College 5, 6-7, 8, 18, 135, 180
Washington, George 2
Washington Grays 37, 39
Washington Literary Society 6-7
Washington Volunteers 38, 39
Watson, E.R. 163
Wayland, B.H. 46
weapons
cannon,34, 47; Colt Patented Firearms Co. 34; Colt-Walker revolver 11; muskets 34, 38, 39, 59; rifles 59; sabres 34
Webster, Daniel 11
Welch, John 37
Welch, Thomas N. 22, 118, 134

Wells, H.H.   141
Whig Party   24, 31, 134, 139, 151
White House (Confederate)   112
White House (U.S.)   166
Whitlock house   60
*Whose Overcoat Have You Got
    On?*   22
Wickham, Williams C.   156, 158
Wigfall, Louis T.   38n
Wilcox, Cadmus M.   52, 61, 63, 66,
    87, 93, 95
Williams, Erasmus   101
Williams, George W.   169
Williams, Lewis B.   40, 42, 43, 49, 89,
    96
Wilmington & Weldon Railroad   79,
    80
Winder, Henry   82
Winn, John J.   38
Wise, Henry A.   19, 24, 26, 28, 30,
    122, 160-161
Wise, John Sargent   160
Withers, Robert E.   139, 141, 150,
    151, 153, 157
Woodson, J.C.   134
Wool, John Ellis   14
Worrell, Joshuah   81
Wright, A.R.   134
Wright, Horatio Gouveneur   115

Y

Yager, Hiram   21
Yancey, William L.   30

About the Author

Harold R. Woodward, Jr. is a native of Madison County, Virginia and a prominent Civil War historian who has written and lectured extensively on Civil War topics. His first book, *For Home and Honor: the Story of Madison County, Virginia during the War Between the States 1861-1865,* was published in 1990.

He is very proud of his family's rich heritage. The first Woodward came to Virginia before 1687, and many of his ancestors served proudly in the Confederate Army.

Mr. Woodward is the current commander of the Kemper-Fry-Strother Camp No. 19, Sons of Confederate Veterans, and is also the commander of the Fourth Brigade, Virginia Division, S.C.V. He is vice president of the Madison Heritage Foundation, a member of the Civil War Society and the Fort Delaware Society, and an honorary member of the Madison Chapter United Daughters of the Confederacy.

A Madison County businessman, Mr. Woodward is active in civic and community affairs. He is currently serving his second term on the Madison County Board of Supervisors.